Papering
& Painting

Julian Cassell
Peter Parham

TIME
LIFE
BOOKS

Alexandria, Virginia

TIME LIFE INC.
President and CEO Jim Nelson

TIME-LIFE TRADE PUBLISHING
Vice President and Publisher Neil Levin
Senior Director of Acquisitions and Editorial
Resources Jennifer Pearce
Director of New Product Development
   Carolyn Clark
Director of Trade Sales Dana Coleman
Director of Marketing Inger Forland
Director of New Product Development
   Teresa Graham
Director of Custom Publishing John Lalor
Director of Special Markets Robert Lombardi
Director of Design Kate L. McConnell
Project Manager Jennie Halfant

Originated in Singapore by Chroma Graphics.
Printed and bound in China by Excel Printing.
10 9 8 7 6 5 4 3 2 1

Front cover photography: **John Freeman** (top and
centre) **Elizabeth Whiting & Associates** (bottom
left and bottom right) **Tim Ridley** (bottom centre)
Back cover photography: **Tim Ridley**

Library of Congress Cataloging-in-Publication Data
Cassell, Julian.
Papering and painting: the essential guide to home
decorating / Julian Cassell & Peter Parham.
   p. cm. — (Time-Life do-it-yourself factfile)
Includes index
ISBN: 0-7370-0310-3 (spiral bound: alk. paper)
1. House painting—Amateurs' manuals. 2.
Paperhanging—Amateurs' manuals. 3. Do-it-yourself
work. 1. Parham, Peter. II. Title. III. Series.

TT323 .C3725 2000
698'.14—dc21   99-089109

Marshall Editions
Project Editor Felicity Jackson

Designed by Martin Lovelock & John Round

Photographer Tim Ridley

Illustrations Chris Forsey

Project Manager Nicholas Barnard

Managing Art Editor Patrick Carpenter

Managing Editor Antonia Cunningham

Editorial Director Ellen Dupont

Art Director Dave Goodman

Editorial Coordinator Ros Highstead

Production Anna Pauletti

Indexer Hilary Bird

Note

Every effort has been taken to ensure that all information in this book is correct and compatible with
national standards generally accepted at the time of publication. This book is not intended to replace
manufacturer's instructions in the use of their tools and materials—always follow their safety guidelines.
The author and publisher disclaim any liability, loss, injury or damage incurred as a consequence, directly
or indirectly, of the use and application of the contents of this book.

CONTENTS

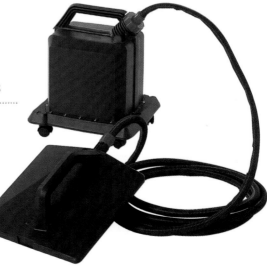

INTRODUCTION

P aper and paint are the primary adornments for home decorating, and creating color schemes using these essential materials can be very rewarding—both conceiving the actual design ideas and the practical application of these ideas to rooms and surfaces within your home. Decorating is an ideal vehicle for self-indulgence since it allows you to express your personal tastes and preferences in a way that is beneficial to your lifestyle by making pleasant surroundings to live in, and beneficial in a practical way by improving the look of your home and adding to its financial value. Experienced decorators and novices alike will benefit from the techniques and advice in the following chapters, because there is always room for improvement, whatever the level of your ability. Trying different techniques and finishes, or experimenting with alternative products, is all part of the process. Painting and papering provide the finishing touches to your home, so enjoy the process and it will continue to give pleasure for many years.

CHOOSING COLOR AND PATTERN

Style is very much a personal issue and the way you choose colors and patterns for your home is based on where you look for inspiration. Most of us have favorite colors and types of design, but molding these into a finished product suitable for your particular room or rooms can be a daunting process. The best thing to do is to seek your inspiration from all areas of life; for example, using lifestyle magazines for ideas and fashion hints can be very helpful. Develop these external influences still further by noting the kind of things that attract you to certain rooms in other people's houses. Look at the variety of shapes and sizes that you come across in your everyday life, and consider how you could apply them to color schemes and designs within your home. Devising a scheme can be as simple or as complicated a process as you wish to make it. By taking into account all the different influences open to you, choosing color and pattern provides an open avenue to fulfilling your desire to create a well-decorated and attractive home.

THE PLANNING PROCESS

The most important part of any papering or painting job is the initial planning stage. The time spent choosing a scheme and preparing the surfaces will always pay dividends by helping to ensure a well-finished product. Chapter 1 provides all the information needed to deal with this stage of the decorating process, demonstrating the most efficient preparatory techniques to use on different surfaces.

ESSENTIAL PAINTING

Applying paint to walls and woodwork in the correct manner is an essential part of the decorating process. Different painting tools require different techniques, so choosing the tools that suit you, and are appropriate for the job at hand, is a matter of personal preference. Chapter 2 provides detailed instruction on using painting tools in the best way possible to ensure that your painted finish will live up to expectations.

CREATING EFFECTS

Paint effects are definitely the fun part of painting, as well as being the decoration that can produce the most dramatic finishes. The processes of producing these stunning effects have a learning curve, with some of the techniques being more difficult than others. Chapter 3 guides you through the various paint effects, plus some modern variations on the more traditional decorating themes, all of which combine to create an exciting, idea-provoking section of this book.

PAPERING PRINCIPLES

Chapter 4 explains the principles and basic methods involved in general paperhanging technique. The success of any papered finish is built on these firm foundations, and progress is dependent on a good grasp of these simple but effective methods. As well as providing instruction on paperhanging, this section also shows you how to solve all the common wallpapering problems experienced by most amateur home decorators.

AWKWARD AREAS

Most rooms are not completely square, and nearly all have some obstacles that need to be overcome during the paperhanging process. Chapter 5 deals with all these areas and provides clear instruction on the best methods to use, from how to deal with arches to building steady and secure platforms for decorating stairwells. A good understanding of these methods will help any decorator deal with the various problems and obstacles encountered on a wall surface.

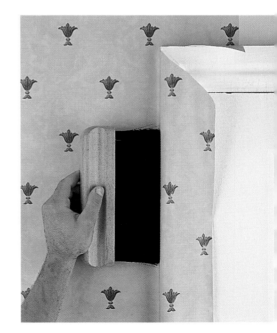

PAINT AND PAPER COMBINATIONS

Most decorative schemes can be enlivened by combining wallpaper and paint to create highly innovative finishes. Chapter 6 discusses the ways of using paper and paint in a scheme, as well as explaining how to apply paintable papers, which give further options to the home decorator. Combining these media can be a very rewarding process, leading to all sorts of highly original decorative finishes and designs.

MODERN INNOVATION

As well as perfecting both the simple and more advanced techniques involved in papering and painting your home, it is a good idea to investigate the innovations and developments in the area of home decoration. Manufacturers are constantly trying to produce new and better materials, which are often claimed to be revolutionary and essential for all enthusiasts. Usually the claims are exaggerated, but sometimes new products do make life much easier and it is worthwhile trying them out. For example, the introduction of rollers for painting was truly a groundbreaking event! Also, water-based paints are becoming by far the most popular paints to use because of their improved formula and ease of use. So, be aware of change and use it to your advantage—finding a new tool for a job, or even refining old techniques and improving them, can be a very enjoyable part of the paint and papering process.

Preparation and Planning

PREPARATION AND PLANNING

1

*Good initial preparation will make the entire
process of decorating easier and help you to achieve
the best possible finish. As well as the physical
preparation required to make surfaces ready for
decoration, it is also essential to plan your
decoration. Choosing color schemes and deciding
on finishes are the essential first steps of any
decorating job; take time to think over all the
options before making any final decisions. This
chapter covers all these aspects and provides a firm
base or starting point on which to build your
painting and paperhanging techniques—it discusses
the many different surfaces
in the home and the best
way to prepare them
for decoration.*

TOOLS AND EQUIPMENT

W hatever the decorating task, the correct tools for the job will help you achieve the best possible finish, so don't compromise on the equipment requirements. Using tools specifically designed for a particular job also makes that job far easier to carry out. Not all the decorating tools are required for every task—a papering and painting toolbox can be built up gradually over time, according to need.

PAINTING EQUIPMENT

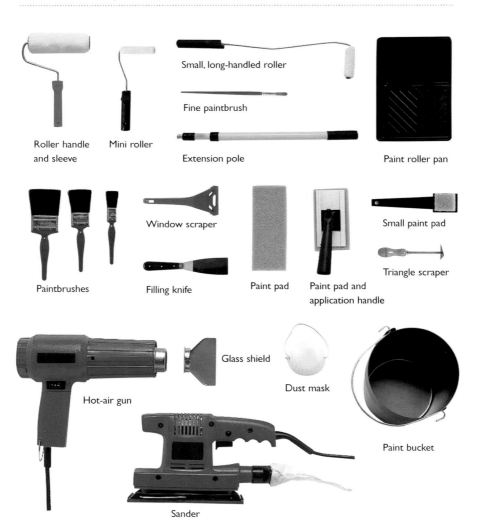

Roller handle and sleeve

Mini roller

Small, long-handled roller

Fine paintbrush

Extension pole

Paint roller pan

Paintbrushes

Window scraper

Filling knife

Paint pad

Paint pad and application handle

Small paint pad

Triangle scraper

Hot-air gun

Glass shield

Dust mask

Paint bucket

Sander

WALLPAPERING EQUIPMENT

Seam roller

Craft knife

Pasting table

Bucket

Wallpaper scorer   Tape measure   Abrasive paper

Pasting brush

Caulking gun

Wallpaper trough

Paperhanging brush   Caulking blade   Sponge

Spirit level

Paperhanging scissors

Rubber gloves

Stepladder

Steam stripper   Protective goggles

CHOOSING A COLOR SCHEME

C hoosing the color scheme for a room can be a difficult process because so many factors have to be taken into consideration. Personal taste should always be the main factor, but you also need to have some awareness of the effects of different colors and patterns and take these into account. Allow enough time at this essential planning stage and consider all the available options and alternatives before making a final decision.

THE COLOR WHEEL

All colors are created from the three primary colors—red, yellow, and blue—with secondary and tertiary colors derived from these. The color wheel below gives an indication of the way in which different colors relate to each other: how they can complement or contrast according to the effect you want.

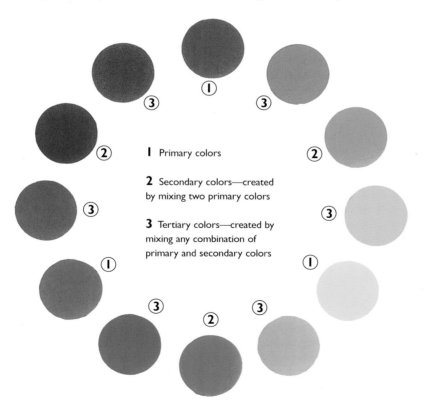

I Primary colors

2 Secondary colors—created by mixing two primary colors

3 Tertiary colors—created by mixing any combination of primary and secondary colors

LIGHT AND COLOR
Color choices should be checked in both natural daylight and artificial light whenever possible, as light can change some colors very dramatically.

THE EFFECTS OF COLOR

- There is no need to understand complicated color chemistry when creating a scheme, simply use the color wheel as a guide.
- Complementary colors: the colors that complement each other sit opposite each other on the color wheel. Combined in a color scheme, they produce a very balanced effect.
- Adjacent colors: using colors that appear next to each other on the color wheel creates a very harmonious scheme with no strong clashes of color.

BALANCED SCHEME
A balanced scheme is one in which no one color dominates the others. In this room, the bright colors complement each other.

PLANNING A SCHEME

- The actual planning of a scheme is affected by a number of factors, such as whether you are using paint or wallpaper. Wallpaper generally means that pattern will play a major role in the scheme, whereas paint on its own places more emphasis on large areas of a single color.
- Focusing the scheme: choosing one color and building the rest of the decoration around it is a common method of producing a scheme.
- Practicality: busy areas of the home receive the most wear and tear—

make sure the scheme you choose will stand up to the treatment it is likely to receive. Expensive, delicate wallpapers, for example, are not ideal for bathrooms or kitchens.
- Furniture and surroundings: a color scheme does not just involve walls, ceilings, and woodwork—flooring, furniture, and other accessories will all have to fit into the final plan. Consider the color and design of all these items and check whether they will complement the ideas and color changes you have in mind.

PROPERTIES OF PAINT AND PAPER

Once colors and designs have been chosen, it is essential to have some understanding of the actual makeup of decorating materials in order to judge whether a particular surface is suitable for the finish you want to achieve. Some wallpapers, for example, require specific treatment; whereas with paint, it is important to apply the correct type for the surface in question.

Types of paint: the majority of paints can be divided into two main types—the more traditional oil-based/solvent-based paints and the water-based/acrylic paints. Oil-based paints are much less user friendly because of their longer drying times and unpleasant smell. They are also more harmful to the environment. For this reason, water-based paints have become increasingly popular and now dominate the marketplace. Oil-based paints used to be considered the most durable, but water-based paints have improved so much that they now match their oil-based counterparts. However, in certain cases, it is still better to use oil-based paints, and these situations are discussed in the following chapters.

PAINT AND ITS USES

- Primer: this type of paint is used to seal surfaces before applying more coats of paint. All bare wood, metal, and other untreated surfaces require priming, otherwise subsequent coats will not adhere properly.
- Undercoat: this is any coat of paint that comes between the primer and top coat on a new surface. It is also used on old painted surfaces before a top coat is applied.
- Eggshell: oil-based paint that provides a dull, almost matte finish. Ideal on wood and can be used on walls for a hardwearing finish. Eggshell hybrids bridge the gap between a totally matte finish and a high-gloss one.

- High gloss: the hardest-wearing oil-based top coat paint, providing a shiny finish. Ideal for wood.
- Latex paint: many different varieties are available. Some include vinyl, which produces a slightly shiny, wipeable finish. Various proprietary latexs have specific properties, ranging from totally smooth finishes to textured ones. Easy to use and ideal for all large surface areas.
- Natural finishes: these translucent paints are used to highlight the natural grain of wood. Stains and varnishes are the best-known ones, although there are now many other different varieties of finish available.

WALLPAPER AND ITS USES

- Plain lining paper: off-white in color, this paper is often used as an alternative to plastering walls that are uneven, because it creates a smooth, sound surface. It can be used as the base for some wallpaper finishes, by being applied to walls and then allowed to dry thoroughly before the final wallpaper is applied over the top; and it can also provide a good base for painting.
- Paintable papers: as well as lining papers, there are other types of textured wallpaper specifically designed to be painted. Woodchip paper is the most common example.
- Vinyl: this is a very popular wallpaper that is ideal in all areas of the home, providing an easily wipeable surface. The hardwearing properties vary according to the grade of vinyl.
- Standard patterned wallpaper: again, very popular and manufactured in many different varieties. Because it is not as durable as vinyl, it is best used in areas like the living room, rather than the kitchen.
- Handmade and hand-painted paper: this is only available in quantity from specialist stores. It is often extremely expensive, but can produce a breathtaking finish.
- Proprietary variations: there are various other papers that may require the use of a specific paste. Always follow the manufacturer's guidelines for these papers, especially if they contain natural fibers such as silk or burlap.

Types of wallpaper: the vast majority of wallpaper falls into two categories: vinyl and standard patterned paper. Vinyl is more hardwearing because of its protective coating. Most wallpaper is hung on the wall using the same technique, though there are small refinements with some papers. The important difference between wallpapers is the method by which they are pasted (see Chapter 4). The main thing at this stage is choosing the correct paper for the purpose (see above), and understanding the effect that a finish may have on a room.

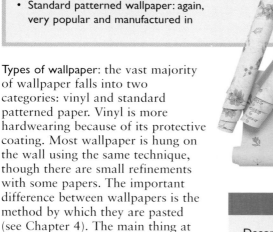

CAUTION

Decorating materials sometimes contain hazardous chemicals that can be damaging to health. Always obey the basic rules of decorating by ensuring good ventilation in the work area, and carefully follow the manufacturer's safety guidelines for whichever product you are using.

PREPARING THE ROOM

The first stage of the practical side of room decoration is preparing the room itself. Having plenty of space to work in, and ensuring that there are no obstacles in the way, is essential when carrying out any papering or painting task. As well as making it easier to carry out the work, a well-prepared room speeds up the job and ensures that it is completed with the least inconvenience in the quickest time possible.

CLEARING THE ROOM

Ideally, everything should be removed from the room you are planning to decorate. If this is not be possible, there are a number of compromises you can make.

- Carpets: if the carpet is going to be changed, this is the time to remove it. Otherwise, it can be taken up and relaid after decoration, or drop cloths can be put down to protect it during the work. If using drop cloths, stick masking tape around the baseboard/carpet junction, to protect the carpet from paint spray.

- Furniture: remove as much furniture as possible. A few heavy items can be moved into the center of the room and covered, but always ensure that all wall surfaces are clear of obstructions.

- Ornaments: take as many as possible out of the room and store them elsewhere until the decorating is finished. Some larger items can be put underneath furniture in the center of the room, but the majority of items should always be removed from the working area.

Covering furniture: use transparent plastic drop cloths for furniture. These protect totally from paint spray, but allow you to see what is under the drop cloth, which is important if any of the items are breakable.

Covering floors: always use good-quality, fabric drop cloths on the floor—cheaper ones let paint through—and make sure they are laid right up to the wall.

IDENTIFYING PROBLEMS

All surfaces require preparation before decoration; once the room is clear, it is much easier to identify the areas that require the most preparation.

Ceiling cracks that follow a relatively straight path are often caused by movement of the building boards used in the ceiling construction. Line ceilings where this occurs, as the cracks will quickly return if you only use filler.

Cracks along ceiling/wall junctions are generally due to settlement in new buildings. Most cracks are due to only slight movement and should be filled with a flexible filler. In older buildings, if the cracks widen, you may need professional advice to check for more serious movement.

Cracks at the corners of windows and doors are often due to slight movement when opening and closing them. Fill with all-purpose filler.

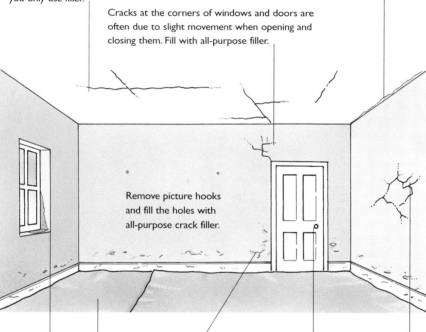

Remove picture hooks and fill the holes with all-purpose crack filler.

Look out for areas of damp, especially around windows. These may need exterior treatment before decoration begins. Alternatively, the damp could be due to condensation.

Scrapes and knocks are part of everyday life. Use all-purpose filler to make good.

Be sure to cover the entire floor with drop cloths.

If the door hardware is to be replaced, now is the time to remove it. Fill redundant screw holes in readiness for fitting the new door hardware.

Cracks that form irregular shapes such as this often suggest that the plaster on old lath-and-plaster walls may be separating from the wall. Tap it with your hand to see if it sounds hollow. If this is the case, the plaster in that area will need to be removed and patch plaster applied.

PREPARING WALLS

Making sure that wall surfaces are smooth before the application of paint or paper plays an important part in achieving a good finish. Lumps and bumps or depressions in the wall surface will be accentuated by the new decoration and spoil the overall look. The amount of preparation will depend on the wear and tear that the walls have received since the last time they were decorated. In many cases, lightly sanding, cleaning, and adding some filler in one or two places may be all that is required. If damage is more extensive, it may be necessary to replaster some areas. Remember that if your walls have old wallpaper coverings, these must be removed before further preparation can start (see pages 24–25).

PATCH PLASTERING

Plastering is a highly skilled trade and, as a rule, attempting to plaster entire rooms on your own should be avoided—it makes far more sense to employ professional help. However, small localized areas that require only slightly more than simple all-purpose filler can be patch plastered—a job well within the capability of the home decorator. Make sure you buy "one-coat plaster," which is easier to work with than the more traditional two-coat plastering systems. Mixed to the manufacturer's guidelines, it takes on the consistency of a stodgy, but easily workable paste.

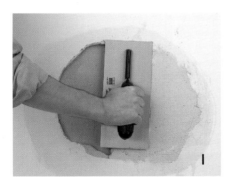

1 Dust away any loose debris from the sides of the hole, and dampen the area by brushing on a coat of general-purpose builder's sealant. Use a plastering float to press the plaster firmly into the hole while drawing the float across the face of the entire filled hole.

2 Smooth the surface of the plaster and allow it to dry slightly (for about 30 minutes). Then wet the face of the float with water and smooth the plaster surface again. Continue "polishing" the surface of the plaster with the float until a smooth and flush finish is produced.

REPAIRING A PLASTERBOARD WALL

Plasterboard or drywall paneling require a different technique in order to fill any holes in the surface layer of the drywall. Because the wall is hollow, plaster or filler will simply fall inside the wall cavity if it is applied directly to the hole. For large holes, a section of drywall may need to be replaced; for smaller holes, the technique demonstrated here is the ideal solution.

1 Use a craft knife to cut away any loose material from around the edge of the hole.

2 Cut a new piece of drywall, slightly larger than the hole. Drill a hole in the center of it and thread a piece of string through it, knotting it on one side. On the opposite side, spread all-purpose adhesive around the edge of the piece of drywall.

3 Holding the string, drop the piece through the hole and move it into place on the reverse side of the hole. Tie the string to a small piece of wood to hold the drywall piece in place.

4 Leave the adhesive to dry, then cut the string away and fill the gap in the wall with plaster.

Minor hole filling: small depressions and holes can be filled with all-purpose filler applied with a filler knife. Where there are several small holes close to each other, a caulking blade can be used to sweep filler over the entire area, filling all the holes with maximum speed and minimum effort.

PREPARING WOOD

W ood tends to act as the frame to the wall decoration and plays an equal part in the overall look of the room. If a professional finish is to be achieved, wood preparation is as important as wall preparation. Wood surfaces can present more problems than walls, as molded corners and edges can make filling and preparation a slightly more intricate task than the broader open surfaces of the walls.

BEFORE FILLING

Before filling the dents and holes in wooden surfaces, you need to deal with any protruding areas. This takes little time, but it helps to ensure a smooth finished product.

1 Knock in any nails that are sticking out of the wood surface, using a hammer and punch.

2 Paint-bumps on old surfaces can be removed by running a scraper along the face of the wood.

FILLING FLAT SURFACES

All-purpose filler can be used to fill the flatter wooden surfaces. Make sure that it is mixed into a smooth, creamy consistency, with no lumps.

1 Filler shrinks as it dries, so fill holes so that the filler sticks up slightly higher than the hole's edges.

2 Once it is dry, the filler can be sanded by hand, or with an electric sander as shown here.

FILLING JOINTS AND CRACKS

Cracks are commonly found at the junction between wood and walls, as well as in the jointing system of wooden items—such as the edges of panels in doors, or the point at which the casing joins onto the main part of the door frame. In all these cases, you need to use a flexible filler that can cope with the slight movement that most of these areas experience. Flexible filler, or caulking, is dispensed from a tube using a caulking gun.

1 Cut the nozzle of the tube, and pull the caulking gun trigger to allow a thin bead of filler to run along the joint. Keep even pressure on the gun trigger while guiding the nozzle along the joint.

2 While the filler is still wet, use a wetted finger to smooth along the bead surface to give an even and neat finish, ready for painting.

UNPAINTED WOOD

After filling as necessary, previously unpainted wood must be sealed before coats of paint can be applied. This is a two-part process involving the use of a solution that seals wood knots and a primer.

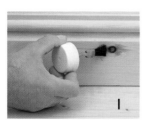

2 Once the knotting solution has dried, seal the entire wood surface with primer, making sure it is totally covered and that the primer is well brushed into the wood.

1 Brush knotting solution into all knots in the bare wood. This seals in any resin and prevents it from bleeding through the coats of paint, which would spoil the surface.

NATURAL WOOD ALTERNATIVES

For natural wood finishes, the wood must be sanded smooth as usual, but use stainable fillers to deal with holes—knotting solution and primer are not usually used on natural wood finishes. Alternative methods are demonstrated on pages 38–39.

PREPARING OTHER SURFACES

A s well as walls and wood, there are other surfaces that require preparation before they can be decorated. The most common of these are metal surfaces and artificial surfaces such as plastic and melamine. With the correct preparation, nearly all of these can be painted to fit in with your chosen color scheme.

METAL SURFACES

The preparation of a metal surface depends very much on the type of metal and whether it has been painted before. There are various all-purpose primers that can be used as a base on most metals, although in many cases it is better to use a primer designed for the specific metal.

PAINTING RADIATORS

Radiators are one of the more common metal surfaces in the home, and they can be painted to either complement or contrast with the rest of the decoration in the room. Because most modern radiators are supplied pre-coated, changing their color is a simple process.

1 Use a fine grade abrasive paper to lightly sand the surface of the whole radiator.

PRIMING METALS

• Copper: there is no need to prime copper—undercoats and top coats can be applied directly to cleaned and sanded surfaces.
• Iron and steel: because these metals are ferrous, they are prone to corroding or rusting. On older surfaces, any old flaky material must be removed. Use a proprietary metal primer before applying more coats of paint.
• Aluminum: generally, proprietary aluminum primers can be used to secure a base coat that may then be painted with top coats.

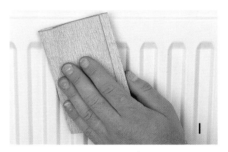

2 Make sure that the radiator is turned off and cool before you paint it. Apply an undercoat and let dry, then paint with a top coat.

MELAMINE

The surface of kitchen cabinet units is often melamine, which is designed not to be painted. However, with recent product developments, it is now possible to paint it, as long as the correct surface preparation is carried out.

1 Clean the melamine surface with a mild detergent solution, rinse with clean water, then leave it to dry completely.

2 Sand the entire melamine surface with a fine grade abrasive paper.

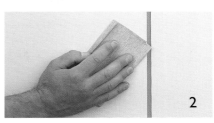

3 Apply a proprietary surface preparation solution to the melamine, wiping it onto all areas with a clean cotton rag.

4 Wipe off the excess solution with another rag and leave to dry. The melamine surface is now ready to accept an undercoat, followed by top coats of paint.

OTHER UNUSUAL SURFACES

Various other surfaces around the home can also be painted, though you should always check the manufacturer's guidelines to see if a particular paint is suitable for a specific surface.
- Tiles: clean and sand tiles, then apply a proprietary tile primer before painting them.
- Textured ceiling coatings: with a previously painted surface, apply

latex paint in the usual way. For a new textured coating, seal the surface with diluted latex paint and leave to dry before applying more coats of paint.
- Glass: clean thoroughly, then use proprietary glass paints to create a decorative effect.
- Plastic: clean thoroughly, then apply top coats directly to the surface.

STRIPPING PAPER

I t is always best to remove old layers of wallpaper before carrying out any redecoration. However secure the old paper may appear on the wall, once it is painted or wallpapered over any defects will begin to show, and these will ruin the look of the newly decorated room.

REMOVING THE WORST

Begin by simply removing those layers of paper that come away from the wall surface with relative ease—starting with any loose seams.

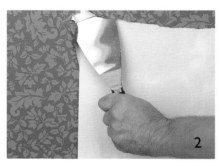

1 The top layer of paper can often be pulled away from its backing, especially when it is vinyl paper.

2 Use the scraper to get behind the paper and remove areas that are no longer stuck to the wall surface.

SIMPLE STRIPPING

Using warm water is frequently the best method of stripping paper that is still stuck to the wall after the top layer has been removed. Do not use this method if vinyl paper is still on the wall, since the water will simply run off the surface.

1 Apply plenty of warm water to the paper. Let the water soak in and make the paper bubble.

2 Scrape away the damp, loosened paper, trying not to dig the edges of the scraper into the wall surface.

USING A STEAM STRIPPER

For stubborn areas of paper, a steam stripper is the best removal tool. The design of steam strippers varies, but in general they combine a large water heating reservoir that boils the water and pushes steam down a connecting pipe into a large plate held against the wallpaper surface.

1 Make sure that the steam stripper is turned off, then fill the reservoir with hot water up to the indicated level. Using hot water speeds up the time it takes for the water to boil. Fit the connecting pipe, then the stripper can be turned on.

2 To speed up the process, score the surface of the wallpaper. Use a scorer to make small holes in the top layer of the wallpaper surface so that steam can penetrate behind the paper and speed up its removal.

3 Once the steamer has boiled, hold the steaming plate flat on the wall surface, keeping it in position for several seconds.

4 Move the plate along and remove the previously steamed piece of paper with a scraper. The time this takes depends on the type of paper and how many layers there are.

CAUTION

Always wear protective equipment when using a steam stripper. Gloves and goggles should both be worn to protect from the steam.

STRIPPING WOOD

Unlike wallpaper stripping, which is usually a necessity before redecoration, stripping wood is not always essential. However, if you are going to apply a natural wood finish to a previously painted surface, or there are layers of old coatings, you need to strip the wood.

HOT-AIR GUNS

Hot-air guns remove paint by heating up the old paint on the surface. This makes it bubble and loosen its grip so it is easy to scrape away.

Using a hot-air gun: hold the nozzle of the gun close to, but not touching, the painted surface. As soon as the paint begins to lift, scrape it away and move the nozzle to a new area, so you do not scorch the wood.

CAUTION

Wear protective gloves and always read the manufacturer's guidelines before using a hot-air gun.

CHEMICAL STRIPPERS

Chemical strippers can be used on paint or natural wood finishes with equal effect. Using this kind of stripper can be a messy business, but it is a very effective way of removing old coatings.

1 Wearing protective gloves, apply chemical stripper liberally to the wood using an old paintbrush.

2 Let the chemical stripper react with the old coatings, then gently scrape away the residue.

PASTE STRIPPERS

Paste strippers are a form of chemical stripper that is particularly suitable for intricate areas that require total coating removal. They take longer to react with the old coatings, but can remove a number of layers with one application. They are messy, so make sure that all areas are covered with drop cloths.

1 Apply the stripper to the surface using a scraper or filling knife. Cover the area to be stripped with an even layer of the paste and leave it on for up to 24 hours to allow it to react with the painted surface.

2 Use a scraper to peel away the paste and reveal the bare wooden surface below. The stripper works by both dissolving the paint and lifting layers away at the same time.

CLEANING WOOD

After any stripping process, wood will require a thorough clean before it can be redecorated. As well as washing with water, it may be necessary to use other solvents, depending on the type of stripper you are using. White vinegar is often used to neutralize the stripper residue, but always check the stripper manufacturer's guidelines on specific recommendations.

1 Wearing protective gloves, wash the entire surface to remove the remnants of previous coatings and any stripper residue.

2 Any ingrained areas of paint can be removed by rubbing a small ball of fine-grade steel wool across the affected area.

SEALING SURFACES

O nce surfaces have been stripped and cleaned, you may need to seal them before they will accept paint or paper. In addition to the wood, metal, and miscellaneous surfaces discussed in this chapter, walls, ceilings, and the larger areas of the room as a whole need sealing to stabilize them before they are decorated.

SEALING CHECKLIST

- Previously wallpapered walls: once the paper has been stripped, the walls should be filled and prepared as usual. The surface should then be sealed with a general-purpose builder's sealant. If wallpaper is going to be used on old, unsound walls, they can be lined first. Walls that are going to be painted, may also require lining first if they are very rough.
- Previously painted walls: after filling and preparing, walls can be painted immediately. If they are to be wallpapered, apply a general-purpose builder's sealant to the surface before proceeding.
- Previously paper-lined walls: ones that have been painted can be

painted again after general preparation. Wallpaper can be applied directly to a wall as long as the lining paper is stuck down. However, it is better to seal the walls with a general-purpose builder's sealant first.
- New plastered walls: they should be sealed with a diluted latex paint (10 parts paint to one part water) before more coats are applied. For wallpaper, walls should be prepared and sealed with a general-purpose sealant, or dilute wallpaper paste (mixed as per manufacturer's guidelines for size), before you proceed.
- New dry-lined walls: these should be treated like new plastered walls.

DEALING WITH STUBBORN STAINS

Standard primers and sealants cannot deal with all the stains that appear on walls and woodwork in the home. Sometimes a more robust form of sealant is required to deal with any areas that continue to bleed a stain through the decorated surface.

Using a stain blocker: apply two or three light coats of aerosol stain blocker to stubborn areas of staining that refuse to disappear even after the usual sealing or priming. Then decorate the surface as usual.

Painting Techniques

PAINTING TECHNIQUES

When it comes to actually applying paint to the walls, painting techniques are often considered with a certain amount of indifference, and this attitude can lead to mistakes that are not easy to rectify. Having prepared surfaces thoroughly, the actual painting part of decorating can be very enjoyable as long as you take the time to ensure that paint is applied correctly. Modern tools make painting a relatively straightforward job, but there are lots of ways of applying paint and it is important to choose an appropriate method for the surface in question and the finish you are trying to achieve.

WHAT TOOLS TO USE WHERE

D ifferent painting tools are designed for particular surfaces, although some tools can be used for more than one type of surface. Most home decorators develop preferences for certain tools and tend to use their favorites as much as possible. However, there are some points that are worthwhile considering when choosing the tools for the job, since they can affect the speed and efficiency of the work.

CHOOSING TOOLS

The table below sets out the advantages and disadvantages of available painting equipment to help you select the right tools for the particular painting job.

PAINTING EQUIPMENT	
Brushes	These are the most versatile of all decorating tools, manufactured in all shapes and sizes, and designed for every possible need. Pure bristle brushes are still the best quality, although some of the modern synthetic-fiber brushes are constantly improving in their performance—especially for use with water-based paints. Brushes can be used successfully in all areas, although for large expanses of ceiling or walls other methods provide much quicker coverage.
Rollers	These are ideal for dealing with large open areas, covering surfaces quickly and with great efficiency. They are manufactured in sheepskin (the best quality) and synthetic materials. Sizes range from about 18 inches (45 cm) down to about 1 inch (2.5 cm), so it is possible to find the right size roller for any job.
Paint pads	These are the direct competition to rollers, as they have very similar properties—it's usually a matter of personal preference. Paint pads create far less mess than rollers, and there is some suggestion that they are much more efficient on paint use than rollers.
Sprayers	These are very successful at covering large surfaces quickly, but the mess created, and the amount of masking off that is required, often makes them too inconvenient. They are useful for large areas of uninterrupted wall space, otherwise they are more suited to industrial painting. However, aerosol spray-can paints are becoming increasingly popular—they are easily directed into inaccessible areas and require no cleaning as they are simply thrown away when empty.

AREAS OF USE

The illustration below shows the different areas of a standard room design and indicates which painting tools are most suitable to use.

Large rollers or large paint pads are ideal for ceilings and walls. Paint pads tend to cause less mess. However, it will still be necessary to cut in around the edges of walls and ceilings using a 2–3-in (5–7.5-cm) brush or small paint pad.

Radiators can be painted with a brush or sprayed with an aerosol. A small, long-handled roller can be used for painting behind them.

Doors can be painted with mini rollers, but the panel edges and frames need finishing with a 1–2-in (2.5–5-cm) brush.

2

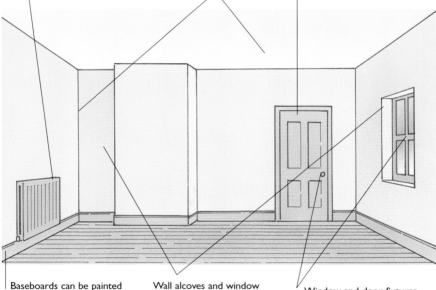

Baseboards can be painted with a medium-size paint pad or a 1–2-in (2.5–5-cm) paintbrush.

Wall alcoves and window recesses are usually too small to accommodate a roller and need to be painted with a 3-in (7.5-cm) paintbrush or a medium-size paint pad.

Window and door fixtures that require painting should be removed and sprayed with aerosol paint. If you don't want to spray with an aerosol, use a fine paintbrush.

KEEPING UP-TO-DATE

It is worthwhile being aware of new paint tools that come on the market since the manufacturers constantly vary shape and design of painting tools in an effort to improve their performance and, ultimately, the finish they produce. Be careful, though, because it is easy to fall into the trap of buying gimmicky tools, which sometimes promise more than they are capable of delivering.

BRUSHES

T he correct technique for using a brush varies slightly according to the surface being painted and the type of paint you are using. Make sure that the brush is in good condition with no loose bristles, which could molt and end up on the painted surface.

WALL TECHNIQUE

To save time, use a relatively large brush when painting walls. However, bear in mind that if your brush is too large, it will be heavy and make your wrist tired, and this may affect your efficiency.

I Apply the paint in random strokes across the wall, allowing the bristles of the brush to spread the paint as evenly as possible.

2 Once a small area of wall has been painted, without reloading the brush, stroke the bristles lightly across the painted surface to blend in any visible brush marks in the paint. This process is known as "laying off."

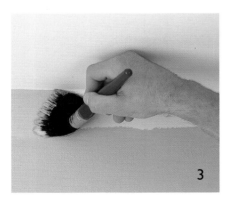

3 Use a smaller brush to cut in around the edges of walls, letting the extreme edge of the brush to "bead" the paint precisely along the wall/ceiling junction.

CUTTING IN

Cutting in is a technique for finishing off around edges, such as those between a wall and ceiling, or the wall and a door frame.

WOOD TECHNIQUE

The same aim of producing a smooth finish applies to painting wood, but the technique varies slightly from that used for walls. If you are using an oil-based paint, make sure that you apply a few more strokes to each paint application so the paint is thoroughly "brushed out," otherwise it may run or drip.

1 Use a smaller brush for wood application since the work always tends to be more detailed. Working in small areas, apply vertical strips of paint, loading the brush separately for each strip. For the door shown here, three strips cover the width of the panel in the door. Without reloading the brush, blend the strips together by stroking horizontally across the painted area.

2

2 Finally, and without reloading the brush, make light vertical strokes over the painted area to remove any brush marks and provide a uniform appearance.

3 For the edges where wood meets walls, such as the baseboard, use a small brush to cut in along the top of the baseboard and create a precise line dividing the two colors.

CLEANING AND STORING BRUSHES

- Temporary storage: wet brushes can be stored temporarily in clinging plastic wrap. Brushes covered with oil-based paint can be stored in a suitable solvent.
- Cleaning: water-based paint should be washed out of brushes with mild detergent, then the brushes should

be rinsed thoroughly under cold water. Wash oil-based paint out of brushes with a suitable solvent, leave them to dry, then wash with a mild detergent and rinse with water.
- Storage: loosely bind the bristles of the brush with brown paper, secured in place with an elastic band.

ROLLERS

R ollers vary in texture and size, but all are extremely efficient at covering flat areas easily and evenly. They are most commonly used on walls and ceilings, although smaller ones and roller sleeves with a very smooth pile can be used on some wooden surfaces.

WALL TECHNIQUE

Large rollers can cover wall surfaces very quickly. Choose a roller sleeve according to the amount of texture you want on the wall—a roller with a thick pile is particularly good if the surface is undulating or uneven. Always load paint evenly onto the roller, being careful not to overload it.

1 Load paint evenly onto the roller, then glide the roller over the wall surface in a zigzag pattern.

2 Reload the roller and fill in the gaps. Glide the unloaded roller gently over the painted area to even up the finish.

EASY ACCESS

Ingenious designs mean that rollers can get into a variety of different areas with relative ease. This easy accessibility makes the roller a very versatile painting tool, which is not confined to straightforward wall spaces.

Gaining height: an extension pole attached to the roller makes it possible to paint the higher areas of a wall without the need for a stepladder. It is also useful for ceilings.

Getting behind: a small, long-handled roller makes it possible to paint behind radiators, or similar obstructions, without removing them from the wall.

WOOD TECHNIQUE

Very similar painting techniques apply to wood and to walls, and rollers are becoming increasingly popular for use on many wooden surfaces in the home, with doors at the top of the list. The main reason for this popularity is the speed at which a roller can paint a door compared to the more traditional methods of paint application.

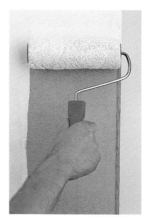

1 For panel doors, mini rollers are ideal for painting all the flat areas on the door surface.

2 Use a paintbrush for the more intricate moldings of the panel edge.

Painting flush doors: a roller is ideal for painting these as there are no intricate areas to interrupt the progress of the roller across the door's surface.

CLEANING AND STORING ROLLERS

- Water-based paints: rollers are designed to be used with water-based paints and can be cleaned with a mild detergent solution before rinsing thoroughly with clean water. This can be a lengthy process, especially with long-pile roller heads, but it is essential to make sure all traces of paint are removed from the roller so that it can be used in the future to apply different colors. Although sheepskin roller heads are more expensive than synthetic

equivalents, they tend to wash out more quickly.
- Temporary storage: rollers can be temporarily stored in plastic wrap for a few days, but should be washed out before this extends to a week.
- Oil-based paint: on the rare occasion that oil-based paint might be used with a roller, it is virtually impossible to clean, and would take far too much solvent. In this case, it is more sensible to use a cheap roller head and throw it away afterward.

PAINT PADS

P aint pads are similar to rollers in that they are designed for covering large surface areas quickly, with relatively little effort and maximum efficiency. Paint pads are flat and rectangular with a large number of tightly packed small fibers, which makes them similar to brushes in the way they convey paint to surfaces. However, paint pads manage to apply the paint very evenly with one sweep of the pad, rather than a number of different strokes. They come in a range of sizes, with large pads designed for painting walls. The precise nature of pad design often means that relatively large pads can also be used for cutting in around edges.

1 Dip the face of the pad in the paint and use the ribbed part of the paint pan to distribute the paint across the pad surface.

2 Remove excess paint from the pad by drawing it across the back edge of the paint pan.

3 Apply paint to the wall using uniform, slightly overlapping strokes across the surface.

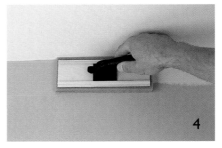

4 Cut in around the wall edges by running the extreme edge of the paint pad precisely along the wall/ceiling junction.

WOOD TECHNIQUE

There is very little difference between the technique used for walls and that used for wood, except that the size of the paint pad needs to be reduced for painting wood. Small paint pads are far more versatile than mini rollers for getting into the detailed parts of wooden surfaces, and they are capable of painting all but the most intricate of areas.

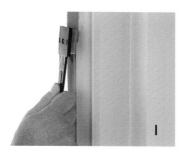

2

1 A small pad is ideal for cutting in along the window-frame trim next to the glass surface. The frame of the pad can be used to guide the fibers precisely along the wood/glass junction.

2 The same-size pad can be used to continue around the outer edge of the window frame, and to cut in along the wall edge.

3 Medium-size pads are ideal for painting a baseboard, but make sure that the profile of the baseboard is not too detailed for the pad surface to mold into.

3

CLEANING AND STORING PAINT PADS

Paint pad fibers are very small and this means the pad itself retains little paint once unloaded. Because the fibers dry very quickly, they must be cleaned immediately after use.

• For water-based paints: remove the pad from its frame and wash it out with mild detergent, then rinse with clean water.

• For oil-based paints: it is nearly impossible to remove all traces of

paint with solvent, so the pad is best discarded after use.

• Temporary storage: paint pads can be stored temporarily in plastic wrap, but this can damage the fibers unless they are wrapped up very carefully. Because they are easily washed out (when using water-based paints), it is better to clean the pads during any breaks in the work or at the end of the job, as required.

NATURAL WOOD FINISHES

Brushes are the ideal tool for most finishes that are applied to natural wood. Wood stain, especially, requires brushing into the grain, a process that other decorating tools are unable to perform efficiently. Natural wood finishes differ slightly from paint ones in that there is no need for priming the wood or sealing knots before applying the desired finish, although it may take a number of coats of the finish to produce the required look.

2

WOOD STAIN

Wood stain is used to give wood a color different than its natural shade. Stain is best used on untreated surfaces because it penetrates deep into the wood, adding color and bringing out the natural grain. Dark wood cannot be made lighter, so the wood to be stained must be a fairly light color to begin with.

1 Always apply stain following the natural grain of the wood. Make sure that the stain is applied evenly because any drips or areas of over-application will stand out when dry.

2 Treat different sections of the wood as separate entities, being careful to cut in precisely along all the divisions—any overlaps of stain will show through the finish.

Filling holes: use stainable fillers when dealing with holes in natural wood. Alternatively, mix a little of the stain you are using with some all-purpose filler to provide a precise match.

VARNISHING

Varnish is a decorative as well as protective finish, and can be bought in anything from matte to high-gloss varieties. It can be applied directly to bare wood or over some stains to act as an extra protective layer. Traditionally, varnish was transparent; nowadays, colored varieties are readily available.

2

1 Varnish should be applied with the grain, in the same way as wood stain, and brushed well into the wood's surface.

2 Bare wood should be given at least three coats of varnish. Give the wood a light sanding between each coat of varnish.

OTHER TREATMENTS

Although stain and varnish are by far the most popular methods of treating bare wood, there are other alternatives that provide equally impressive finishes.

- Stain/Varnish: this all-purpose finish combines both stain and varnish finishes in one product. Apply in the usual way with a paintbrush.
- Scandinavian oil: this is ideal for hardwoods since it penetrates deep into the wood and nourishes it. Apply with a brush and buff with clean cotton rags.
- Wax: the most traditional of all natural wood finishes. Apply the wax with a cotton rag and buff when dry to reveal the natural beauty of the wood. The one drawback is that waxed surfaces need to be recoated regularly to maintain their sheen.

Combining stain and varnish: you can extend the life of a stained surface, and increase the depth of the finish, by giving it a coat of varnish once the stain has dried.

FINISHING TOUCHES

O nce all the major areas in a room have been painted, it is important to pay attention to the more detailed places that may not initially appear to require any decoration. Adding finishing touches is highly beneficial to the end result, ensuring that the decoration is as good as possible.

2

PAINTING DETAIL

Painting the smaller features in a room requires some variation from the standard techniques already demonstrated in this chapter. As detailed areas have a smaller surface, the tools used to paint them need to be scaled down.

Using aerosols: ideal for getting into intricate areas, aerosol paints can be used on such items as window fixtures. Remove them from the window and spray them on an old board. They may require two or three coats to provide an even finish and, as with all spray painting, it is better to apply several thin coats rather than a few thick ones which will make the paint run.

Painting in situ: some older window or door fixtures may be very difficult to remove from their position. In such cases, it is best to use a fine brush to paint them while they are in place.

Touching up scrapes: small knocks or imperfections on a newly painted surface should be touched up using a fine brush; painting the area with a large brush can sometimes create a rather shadowy finish. Since coats of paint should always be applied to complete surface areas rather than just small details, a detailed dab with a small brush will be less visible.

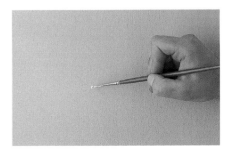

CLEANING DETAIL

Ensuring that all surfaces are clean after painting will add to the finished look. As well as general cleaning, it may be necessary to remove small paint spills.

2

Carpet spills: paint drops can often find their way through drop cloths to the carpet below. Small splashes can be removed by scraping the edge of a craft knife blade across the surface of the paint once it is dry.

Cleaning handles: unpainted window and door hardware may need to have paint splashes removed from their surface. Polishing with a cotton rag will remove most paint spots; or, use a plastic non-scratch scourer.

Glass overspray: paint splashes on glass are usually unavoidable when painting windows. Use a window scraper to remove them.

Electrical sockets: a window scraper is ideal for removing unwanted paint from the surface of electrical sockets. Be careful not to scratch the socket.

CLEANING CHECKLIST

Once the painting is finished, it is a good idea to spring-clean the room to show off the new-look interior.

- Curtains: this is the ideal time to get curtains dry-cleaned, along with cushion covers and any other soft furnishings in the room.

- Windows: clean all windows and other glass.
- Carpets: hire a carpet cleaner to revive older floorcoverings.
- Ornaments and accessories: polish all the odds and ends in the room to add to its new look.

PROBLEM SOLVING

However proficient your painting technique, it is inevitable that you will experience some problems from time to time. Most are easily rectifiable and just require simple preparational work before recoating. Some of the most common problems are outlined below.

2

Drips: these are mainly experienced with oil-based paints, although poor application of water-based paints can also lead to drips or runs. Use a scraper to remove the run, sand the area, and recoat.

Bubbling: this is usually caused by impurities on the bare surface before paint was applied. Sand the area back and seal or prime as required, before recoating.

Bleeding knots: staining on painted woodwork is often caused by a knot that is bleeding sap through the painted surface. Scrape the sap away and sand back to the knot in question. Apply knotting solution, then prime and recoat, as required.

Blotchy stain: overlapping brush strokes on a stained surface can lead to a blotchy, unsightly finish. Sand the entire section of wood right back to bare wood before recoating.

Overlapping: on natural wood finishes, do not overlap wet brush strokes onto a dry area, or the joint will be very noticeable. Maintain a "wet" edge during application. Sand the area back and recoat.

Dust and dirt: a rough or gritty painted surface can be caused by poor preparation (lack of sanding) or a buildup of dirt on the brush that is then transferred to the surface. Sand the area and recoat.

Special Paint Effects

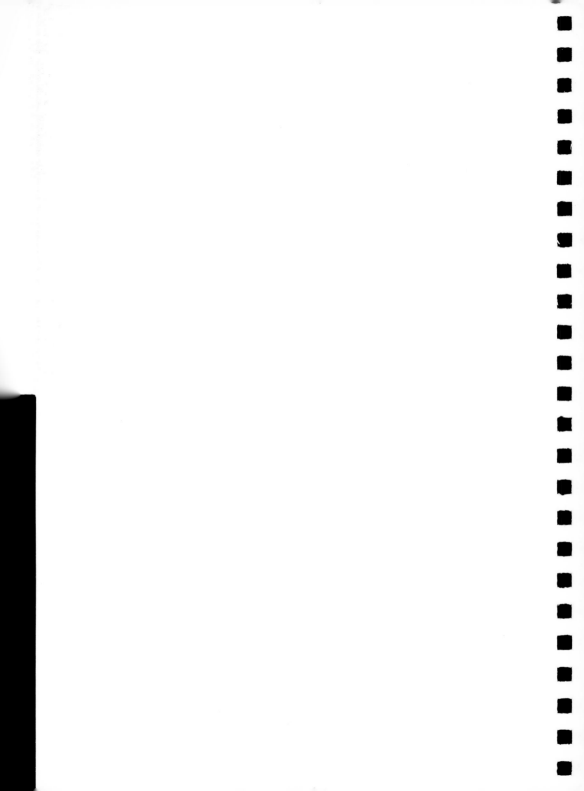

SPECIAL PAINT EFFECTS

Special paint effects are a way of adding extra interest and texture to a wall or wooden surface by applying standard decorating paints or transparent glaze in slightly different ways. All these techniques are aimed at producing a finish that is far removed from a smooth, opaque painted surface. Paint and glaze applied in the ways outlined in this chapter add a totally new dimension to traditional decorating, giving you highly individual, dramatic finishes. Apart from their obvious impact, producing special effects is an incredibly enjoyable and satisfying process, and however proficient you become in a particular technique, every piece of decorative work you produce will be unique and add a personal touch to the decoration in your home.

3

WHAT PAINT EFFECTS TO USE WHERE

Like paint in general, paint effects can be applied to most surfaces. However, some effects are more suited to particular areas than others; the box below will help you plan your effects.

WHERE TO USE PAINT EFFECTS

PAINT EFFECT	IDEAL AREA	COMMENTS
Sponging	Suited to large surfaces.	Avoid use on molded wood.
Ragging	Similar to sponging, it is ideal for large surfaces.	Avoid rooms with too many intricate edges or corners.
Rag rolling	Ideal for walls and panels; difficult around the edges.	If possible, fit baseboards after the paint effect is applied.
Dragging and graining	Well suited to woodwork, intricate or plain.	Can be used on walls, but difficult to keep an even finish.
Color-washing	One of the simplest effects to create on walls.	Effect is called timber rubbing when done on wood.
Liming	Ideal on light-colored, bare wood surfaces.	Similar to timber rubbing, except a lime wax is used.
Marbling	Ideal way of breaking up a wall with "marble" panels.	Difficult effect to achieve, but produces impressive finish.
Aging effects	Excellent way of giving any surface a well-lived-in look.	Includes distressing and crackle varnishing processes.
Stippling	Ideal for walls and woodwork.	Provides a wonderful textured looking finish, but takes time.
Combing	Good on walls as well as panels and woodwork.	Provides a coarser look than dragging and graining.
Stamping	Good on walls.	Good for repeating a design.
Stenciling	Reproduces painted designs on any surface.	Good for creating borders, frames, and other designs.

3

SPECIALIST EQUIPMENT

P roducing paint effects requires a few extra tools. Always buy quality tools, since the extra expense will pay dividends in the work produced.

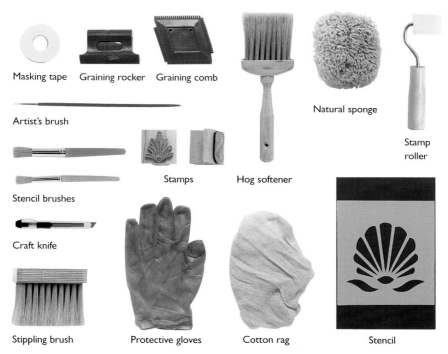

Masking tape   Graining rocker   Graining comb

Artist's brush

Natural sponge

Stamp roller

Stencil brushes

Stamps   Hog softener

Craft knife

3

Stippling brush   Protective gloves   Cotton rag   Stencil

GLAZES

Some paint effects, such as sponging, can be produced with standard latex paint, but in general most effects are produced by using transparent glaze. Adding color to glaze creates the translucent, broken color finish that is characteristic of most paint effects. Traditionally, glazes were oil-based, but now the vast majority available in the marketplace are water-based/acrylic. Water-based glazes tend to be much easier to work with and far more environmentally friendly. All the glazes used in this chapter are water-based, and demonstrate that they are quite capable of producing any effect you require. Mixing the glaze varies according to the manufacturer's guidelines: generally it is a simple case of mixing colorizers with the base glaze until you have the desired color. It is vital to remember that all glazes—and therefore all paint effects—must be applied over a base coat of some description. Some water-based and some oil-based paints can be used, although a vinyl latex paint is often the manufacturer's choice. A light color always works best as the base coat, so that subsequent glaze layers show to best effect.

SPONGING

S ponging is one of the simplest paint effects to produce, while achieving one of the most dramatic finishes. A natural sponge is used to make imprints on the wall surface, creating a finish that combines color, texture, and depth to great effect.

SPONGING ON

Latex paint or glaze can be used for this technique, although glaze will create a far more translucent finish, which is often more appealing. As the name of the technique suggests, the sponge is actually used to apply the glaze to the wall.

1 Place a little glaze on an old paint-container lid. Dip the sponge into the glaze and remove any excess on the rim of the lid or on a piece of scrap paper.

2 Make a number of impressions on the wall before reloading the sponge with more glaze. Alter the angle of the sponge slightly with each new impression.

3 Reload the sponge and begin to fill in the bare areas of wall, gradually building up an even coverage across the wall surface.

4 Once one color is complete, use a second color to build up depth in the design.

SPONGING OFF

This technique differs slightly from "sponging on" in that the glaze is applied directly to the wall first and then a sponge is used to create impressions in the glazed surface. The finish tends to be slightly more subtle than "sponging on," but equally effective in producing depth and texture.

1 Use a brush to apply the glaze to the wall, making brush strokes in random directions and applying even coverage. Only cover an area of up to one square yard (meter) at a time, otherwise the glaze will start to dry in some places before you have the chance to produce the effect.

2 Press a dampened sponge onto the glazed surface, creating a mottled broken color effect. As with sponging on, keep changing the angle at which the sponge comes in contact with the wall, to give a random but even finish.

3

REFLECTING TEXTURE
A sponged-off finish produces a wonderful overall effect, which changes its appearance according to different light intensity.

SPONGING IDEAS

In addition to the standard sponging instructions, the following ideas can be added to the general technique.
- Using different sides: most natural sponges have one side that has a much finer texture than the other. Choose whichever side creates the effect you want, or combine both.
- Creating shadows: vary the intensity of the pattern by making more

impressions near any corners or alcoves—this will produce a very interesting shadowy effect.
- Dealing with corners: cut a small section off a sponge, tape it to the end of a pencil and use this to gain access to internal corners.
- Keeping clean: while producing sponging effects, wash the sponge frequently in plenty of clean water.

RAGGING AND RAG ROLLING

Cotton rags are used in a similar way to sponges to create texture impressions on the wall surface with glaze. Although the technique is similar, the finished effect is very different.

RAGGING ON

Ragging on is similar to "sponging on" in that the rag is used to apply the glaze to the wall. You need to have a plentiful supply of rags at hand, since they soon become too ingrained with glaze to be used effectively.

1 Pour some glaze onto an old plate or paint-tub lid. Crumple the rag in your hand and dip it into the glaze. Remove any excess on the rim of the lid or on a scrap of paper.

2 In a similar fashion to sponging, press the rag onto the wall to create rag impressions. Keep altering the angle at which you apply the rag in order to create a random effect.

RAGGING OFF

This method is used to create a textured impression in wet glaze. Only apply glaze to areas of up to one square yard (meter)—it has a limited working time.

1 Apply the glaze randomly. For a more even finish, you can lay off the glaze in a vertical direction.

2 Press a damp, crumpled rag into the wet glaze, altering wrist and hand angle as you move across it.

RAG ROLLING

Rag rolling extends the principle of using rags by making the impressions that they create much more directional. Rag rolling can be carried out in any direction, but by far the most common method is to use the rags to create vertical, relatively uniform striped patterns. Rag rolling is much more effective using the "ragging off" method, rather than the "ragging on" one.

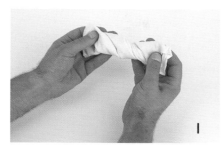

1 Screw up a number of pieces of rag and twist each one into an irregular sausage or finger shape. Make all the sausage shapes roughly the same size.

2 Apply the glaze to the wall, then roll a sausage-shaped rag down the wall surface, creating a tumbling, relatively uniform ragged effect. Make sure that you keep the rag in contact with the wall surface at all times, using a continuous rolling motion as it progresses down the wall. Use a washed-out rag for each subsequent roll down the wall.

RAGGING VARIATIONS

The name "ragging" is used as an all-encompassing term when referring to the technique demonstrated above. In reality, cotton rags are not the only fabrics that can be used to create this paint effect. Try experimenting with any of the items in the following list—each one creates a slightly different, very distinctive variation on the traditional ragged effect:

- plastic bags
- denim
- burlap
- lace
- muslin
- net
- velvet
- corduroy

THE FABRIC LOOK
Rag rolling produces a highly textured fabric look on any wall surface. Although relatively simple to create, it gives the appearance of being extremely complicated.

DRAGGING AND GRAINING

D ragging and graining are both effects that are used to produce a highly textured and directional finish. They can either be applied on a wooden surface to accentuate its texture, or on other surfaces to mimic the grain of wood. Both techniques require practice but, once mastered, the effects you can produce are extremely gratifying.

DRAGGING

Dragging is a good effect to apply to any woodwork—especially panel doors. Special dragging brushes can be used, although good effects can be created with a flogger or softening brush, or even a paintbrush with coarse bristles.

1 Apply the glaze to the door, treating different sections of the door as separate items.

2 Drag the brush through the glaze in the direction of the natural grain of the wood. Make sure that the bristles are at a very acute angle with the surface of the door. The coarseness in texture can be varied with the bristle angle.

3 After each sweep with the brush, remove excess glaze from the bristles with a clean cotton rag.

4 Treat each section of the door as a separate item, creating precise dividing lines between each one.

GRAINING

Graining bears some similarities to dragging, except that a specially designed tool—a graining rocker—must be used to create the desired effect. Graining can be carried out on wooden surfaces or, as in this case, the lower level of a wall can be grained to reproduce a wooden panel effect.

1 Apply the glaze to the wall surface, being careful to lightly smooth it out with vertical strokes of the brush.

2 Starting on the extreme edge of the wall, hold or fix a wooden batten so that it is precisely vertical. Then pull the graining rocker down through the glaze, using the edge of the batten as a guide.

3

3 The rest of the rocker strokes must now be made by eye—the wooden batten would damage the effect as you move across the surface. Make slight rolling motions with the rocker as you drag it through the wet glaze. This technique has the effect of mimicking the wooden knots and variations found in wood grain on the wall surface.

THE PANEL EFFECT
Graining is an extremely effective way of producing a mock paneled look on an otherwise flat, characterless wall surface.

COLOR-WASHING AND LIMING

B oth these effects are aimed at highlighting the features of the base surface below. Whether on walls or wood, the idea is to produce a translucent finish, with the use of color and/or glaze, that accentuates features in that surface.

COLOR-WASHING

A color-wash uses glaze to create a translucent layer over a base coat of a latex or an undercoat paint. Matte latex provides an absorbent base that soaks up the color-wash; a vinyl latex base coat will produce a more subtle look.

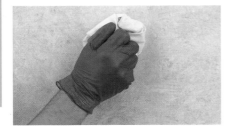

Wiping away: the wash is brushed on and immediately wiped away. This creates a translucent finish with varying degrees of color intensity.

Leaving alone: alternatively, the wash can be applied with random brush strokes and left as the finished effect, creating a color-dominant finish.

TIMBER RUBBING

Timber rubbing can be considered as color-washing on wood. The wood should have no base coat—glaze is applied directly to the untreated surface.

1 As with dragging, treat separate areas of the door as separate items, applying the glaze generously.

2 Use a damp rag to wipe away excess glaze to highlight the grain of the wood with a little glaze color.

LIMING

Liming (or pickling) acts in a similar way to timber rubbing, except that white is the characteristic color produced with the finish, and the actual product used to create the finish is a purpose-designed wax rather than a glaze. It is essential that the wood is untreated before this effect is applied.

1 Open up the grain of the wood by scrubbing it lightly with a wire brush, working in the direction of the grain.

2 Apply generous amounts of the liming wax to the wooden surface using a ball of fine-grade steel wool. Make sure that the wax gets into all areas.

3 Wipe off the excess wax with a cotton rag. It is possible to buff the surface to give it a slight sheen, characteristic of all waxed surfaces.

THE LIMED LOOK

Liming produces a very traditional rustic finish on wood, and limed paneling such as this creates a very restful, comfortable atmosphere. Liming is especially effective when it is combined with natural materials and other aged or distressed paint effects in a room.

MARBLING

Marbling is one of the most difficult paint effects to master: it is an attempt to reproduce the look of a natural substance. It takes a great deal of practice to achieve a really good marble effect, but it is possible to create this most luxurious-looking of all paint finishes. Naturally occurring marble differs hugely in color and appearance, but the marbling method shown here provides an attractive two-color marble effect for the walls in your home.

1 Paint the wall with a white vinyl latex base coat and let dry. Mix two glazes, one a light gray and one with raw umber as the only colorizer. Apply random patches of each glaze with a fine, flat-bristled brush; leave some white areas uncovered.

2 While both the glazes are still wet, use a stippling brush across the entire wall surface to apply a textured effect and blend the two glazes into each other.

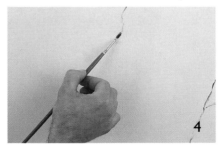

3 Use a softening brush or flogger to stroke gently across the glaze, blending both glazes still further and taking some of the harshness out of the stippled effect. First brush in the direction of the glaze, then across its grain, and then with the flow again.

4 Dip an artist's brush into some raw umber and then into each of the two glazes. Draw the brush across the wall surface while slowly rotating it between thumb and index finger. Keep the veins running in one direction to mimic natural marble.

5 Soften the veins by first brushing in the direction they are running, then across their "grain," and finally with their direction again.

6 Leave the wall to dry completely before applying two or three coats of lacquer.

7 Use a fine-grade abrasive paper to gently sand over the entire surface. Finally, polish the finish using a soft cotton rag.

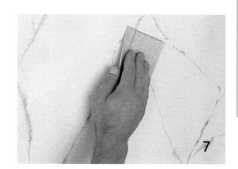

3

LUXURIOUS FINISH
A marbled paint effect is a luxurious finish in its own right—it also makes the wall a dramatic backdrop for ornaments and other display items.

AGING

There are many different ways of aging a decorated surface in order to produce the comfortable, lived-in feel of years of wear and tear. The methods shown here are not the only ones, but they are extremely effective ways of creating this particular look.

DISTRESSING

This technique is particularly effective on wooden paneled surfaces, as a large area displays the finish to best effect. Choose colors carefully when creating a distressed look—it always works best if you have a base color that is a lighter shade than the one used as the top coat.

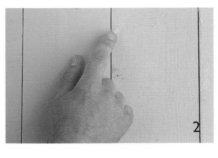

1 Apply the light base coat directly onto the untreated wood surface, and leave it to dry.

2 Where you want the color to show through the top surface, apply random streaks of petroleum jelly, paying particular attention to the edges of the boards with just the odd streak along their central areas.

3 Apply the darker top coat over the entire paneled surface, being careful to cover it totally. Leave the top coat to dry.

4 Sand the panels with fine-grade abrasive paper. Where petroleum jelly was applied, the top coat will not stick; it rubs away to reveal the base color. The degree of distressing depends on the amount of sanding.

CRACKLE GLAZE

There are a number of different crackle finishes, but crackle glaze is one of the most effective ways of producing this aged, antique look. Application methods vary slightly between manufacturers, but the method shown here demonstrates the most commonly used technique for producing a crackle-glaze finish.

1 Apply a base coat to the wall surface. Vivid bright colors work particularly well with this effect; even the base coat should be a strong color, so it emphasizes the finish as clearly as possible.

2 Apply the crackle glaze with a generously loaded brush. It is essential to keep the brush strokes going in the same direction.

3 Thin the top coat of latex paint with one part water to 10 parts paint. Apply it using brush strokes at right angles to each other, never returning to an area once the paint is applied. Slowly but surely the crackle effect will begin to appear.

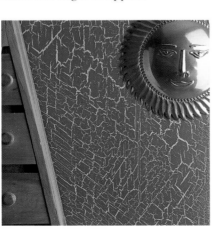

NATURAL CRACKLE
Crackle glaze produces a fascinating "crazed" surface, combining both color and texture to great effect.

STIPPLING

S tippling produces a fine textured effect, and it can be built up in
layers to produce greater depth. Flat, open surfaces are best suited to
stippling, since it is easier to maintain a consistency of texture on them.

1 Apply the glaze to the wall with
slightly swirling brush strokes, in
all directions. Total coverage is not
necessary, as small patches of base
coat will be covered with glaze once
stippling begins.

2 Once an area of one square yard
(meter) has been covered with
glaze, use the stippling brush to make
small impressions on the surface.
Make short dabbing motions, letting
only the very tips of the bristles
come in contact with the wall. Vary
your hand angle as you gradually
progress across the wall. Once one
area is complete, apply more glaze to
the wall and continue to stipple as
before. Remove excess glaze from the
bristles with a clean cotton rag after
each glazed area is complete.

3 Use a stencil brush to complete
the effect in the corner junction
of the wall—it is difficult to gain
access to internal corners with a
stippling brush.

STIPPLING EFFECT
Stippling creates a wonderful warm glow
across a wall surface. Light is refracted from
it with different intensities, producing a truly
three-dimensional finish.

COMBING

A special tool called a graining comb is used on a stippled surface to create this highly textured decorative effect. Combs vary in design, but all produce a directional flow of glaze that combines the base and glaze color to produce a two-tone effect. The comb shown here has differing gaps and sizes of teeth, which can be used to create different grades of effect.

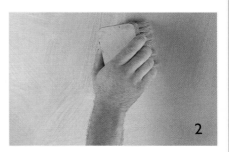

1 Apply glaze in random directions across the wall surface in areas of up to one square yard (meter) at a time, as the glaze has a limited workable time before it dries. Be careful to cover the area totally.

2 For a more even effect, stipple the glaze to give a uniform textured finish. See opposite for the technique of using a stippling brush.

3

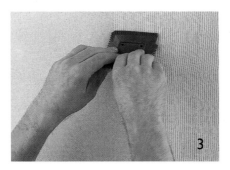

3 Draw the comb down through the glaze to create a grooved effect, removing any excess glaze from the teeth of the comb with a dry rag after each sweep.

VARYING TEXTURE
By combining two sizes of combs, it is possible to create an interesting striped effect such as this one.

STAMPING

S tamping is a quick and easy way of applying and repeating painted images across a wall or wooden surface. The images can be applied singly or in groups, and may be used to create single feature designs or mixed with other stamps to produce a collage effect. Stamps can either be bought or made—the application method remains the same.

HOUSEHOLD OBJECTS

Stamps can be made out of any number of objects found around the home, as long as the item chosen can absorb paint. A small brush can be used to apply paint to a stamp, or you can use a custom-made roller as shown opposite.

Sponges: draw an animal design on a sponge and cut it out using a craft knife. Reloading the sponge after each stamp is not necessary because it is so absorbent.

Corks: bind three corks together with tape to create a cloverleaf design. Reload the corks with paint after each stamp. Make the stem of the leaf with a small, fine brush or by rotating the painted edge of a single cork below the cloverleaf design.

Potatoes: draw a picture on the flat cut half of a potato, then cut out the design with a craft knife. Make sure that the entire surface area of the design is placed in full contact with the wall, then remove it to reveal the impression.

CUSTOM-MADE STAMPS

Although making your own stamps is great fun, manufactured stamps tend to be easier to use and create more defined impressions when applied to the wall. Choose a design that fits in with the particular theme and effect you are trying to create in your room.

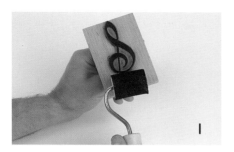

1 Load a small foam roller with the chosen paint color. Apply it to the stamp, ensuring that the entire design is covered. Before applying it to the wall, test the stamp on a piece of scrap paper to check whether you need to remove excess paint from its face before applying it to the wall.

2 Apply the stamp to the wall, making sure that there is full contact between the design and wall surface. Press down firmly.

3 Pull the stamp away from the wall, being careful not to smear the design, and continue to apply more stamps to build up your overall picture. Reload the stamp with paint as required.

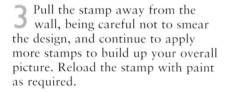

CREATING A THEME
Stamps are ideal for creating a decorative theme in a room—they can be used for a subtle design or a dramatic effect.

STRAIGHTFORWARD STENCILING

S tencils are similar to stamps in that they provide a technique for producing a design motif on a wall or wooden surface. However, the way in which stencils achieve this effect is completely different than the method for stamping. Stencils can be bought or made—making your own gives greater opportunity for personal expression.

MAKING A STENCIL

Stencils can be made out of custom-made cardboard or plastic. Stencil plastic is the most practical choice, since it is easily washed and can be used time and time again with equal accuracy. Stencil designs can either be drawn by hand or traced, and you can use various natural products as the basis for your design.

1 Choose a leaf cluster that demonstrates a strong shape as well as a balanced overall design. Place it on a board, using some tape to hold it in place, if required. Hold some tracing paper over the top of it and use a pencil to trace around the edge of the design.

2 Remove the leaves, and stick the traced image to the board with some masking tape. Hold a sheet of thin stencil plastic over the tracing paper, and use a fiber-tip pen to draw the traced design on the plastic.

3 Remove the tracing paper and stick the stencil plastic to the board with masking tape. Follow the fiber-tip pen guideline to cut out the leaves, stem, and stalk of the stencil design, using a sharp craft knife on a cutting board. The stencil is then ready to use.

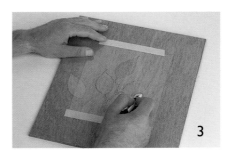

USING A STENCIL

The design below can be used as a border around doors or windows, or as a more overall wall pattern as demonstrated here. Custom-made acrylic stencil paints are the ideal materials to use for filling in the design. For a more imaginative finish, try mixing color with latex paint and colorizers.

1 Use some masking tape to hold the stencil securely in position on the wall surface.

2 When using a stencil brush, load the brush with paint so that the bristles remain relatively dry—the excess paint can be removed by dabbing the brush a few times on a piece of scrap paper to leave just a trace of color on the brush. Brush on the color, using light dabbing motions perpendicular to the wall surface. Vary the color within the design to make it look lifelike.

3 Once complete, remove the stencil carefully to reveal the finished design. Move along to the next area and repeat Steps 1 and 2.

COLORFUL STENCILING
Stencils can produce well-defined images on all manner of surfaces, creating a definite picture or scene that can be kept small or expanded to produce a much larger effect.

CREATING STENCIL EFFECTS

As your technique improves, it is possible to create more specialized effects with stencils. The increased use of color, shading different areas with more paint, or highlighting parts of a stencil more than others, can create a shadow effect that hints at a specific light source and produces a more three-dimensional appearance. Shading more on one side of a stencil gives the effect of direct sunlight and the direction from which it is coming. Alternatively, making the edges of a flower design more pronounced, as shown here, gives a very vibrant lifelike finish to the stencil.

1 Attach the stencil to the wall with masking tape. Increase the color intensity on the extreme edges of the design, while leaving central areas more sparsely colored.

2 Carefully remove the stencil to reveal a textured effect that demonstrates more depth than the more simple stencil techniques.

ALTERNATIVE STENCILING MATERIALS

In addition to standard stencil brushes, it is possible to use various other tools to apply paint to a stencil.
- Sponges: natural sea sponges have a pronounced texture, which makes them ideal for use on large stencils; always make sure you remove the excess paint before applying it.
- Aerosols: as the spray cannot be pinpointed on a small area, aerosol

paints are best used for stencil designs that do not require close color changes. They are very quick to use.
- Crayons: stencil crayons are a good alternative to traditional paints. The sticks can be rubbed on a piece of stencil plastic that can then be used as a palette for transferring paint to the stencil with a stencil brush.

Papering Techniques

4

PAPERING TECHNIQUES

Wallpaper varies in design, pattern, and size, but the actual techniques for applying the different types changes very little. Once you have established a sound basic papering technique, you can hang nearly all types of paper with equal success. This chapter outlines the simple rules and correct techniques for carrying out straightforward wallpapering. Once this stage is mastered, it is simply a matter of refining these techniques for more complicated wallpapering situations. Follow all the necessary preparations outlined in Chapter 1 before beginning to hang the wallpaper, and don't try to hurry the papering process because speed will develop naturally with experience.

4

WHAT PAPER TO USE WHERE

M ost paper can be applied in any area of the home, although some types of wallpaper are more suited to particular rooms than others (see page 15 for the properties of each type of paper). However, it is worthwhile considering the effects of different designs and patterns in conjunction with the use of the room and the style you are trying to achieve.

The formal choice: dining rooms and reception areas are the ideal places to use traditional designs, which can be linked to the period of the property or simply to add a touch of grandeur and style to the room as a whole.

Practical papering: it is best to use vinyl papers in bathrooms and kitchens so that the wall surfaces can be wiped and cleaned very easily. A striped design produces a precise, elegant look that is suited to most areas in the home.

Having fun: children's rooms offer the chance to choose fun designs to create a happy, playful atmosphere.

4

THE EFFECTS OF DESIGN

Different designs on wallpapers can create completely different effects. In much the same way that color can produce a particular feeling within a room, the pattern of the wallpaper can completely alter the atmosphere and mood; when choosing a design always take into consideration the effect that the design in question will have on the room as a whole.

Stripes

Vertical striped wallpapers always create a feeling of height and are therefore ideal for rooms in which you want to give the impression of "raising" the ceiling. Don't use striped wallpaper on uneven walls, as any slight undulations will be accentuated by the clear, sharp lines of the stripes.

All-over effects

Recent fashion has meant that there are a number of papers available that have an all-over, almost paint effect design, such as a color-wash or stippled effect. These wallpapers tend to be easy to hang, but it can be difficult to hide seams since there is no precise pattern to draw your eye away from them. This happens with darker colors in particular, and it is worthwhile considering hanging and painting a lining paper a similar base color to the wallpaper before hanging the wallpaper, so that any slightly open seams will have the appropriate background color.

Floral papers

These are generally easy to hang since they tend to have a fairly busy design that hides the seams easily. Big floral patterns should be hung in large rooms, otherwise the pattern can look cramped and make the room seem smaller than it actually is. Small floral patterns tend to create a country cottage effect, and they are ideal for uneven or slightly rough walls because the busy pattern on the paper draws your eye away from any imperfections in the wall surface.

Singular designs

Wallpapers with one or two motifs repeated time and time again need precise matching—if the paper is not hung exactly vertical, any discrepancies will be very obvious on the wall. While they produce an excellent effect, these papers are not the easiest ones for a beginner to hang.

Papered scenes

Some manufacturers produce papers with landscape designs. The rolls of paper have to be applied to the wall surface in a particular sequence in order to build up a precise picture. This unusual effect can produce an impressive finish in any room as long as the size of the design can be fitted into the available wall space. Similar to these papers are trompe l'oeil paper panels, which can be used to create another faux effect on a wallpapered surface in a room.

Period papers

Some paper designs have a classical appeal that never seems to age over the generations or go out of fashion— the fleur-de-lis design, for example, has been copied for many years and still maintains its popular appeal. Many of these classic designs produce quite a formal decorative effect in a room and this factor should always be taken into consideration when choosing this type of wallpaper.

4

MEASURING, CUTTING, AND PASTING

Ensuring that you have the right number of rolls for the job is obviously an important factor when papering. The way in which these rolls are prepared, cut and pasted, and ready for wall application is also essential in producing the required finish. Whatever type of paper is being used, the dimensions of the room must be measured accurately.

CALCULATING THE NUMBER OF ROLLS

A simple way of calculating the number of rolls required for a room is shown below. Manufacturers usually state the size of the pattern repeat on the roll label, but it is worthwhile checking it yourself.

$$\frac{\text{Height of room} + \text{Wallpaper repeat size} \times \text{Distance around baseboard}}{\text{Area of one roll}} = \text{Number of rolls required}$$

AREA OF ONE ROLL

Most wallpapers are about 11 yd (10 m) long by 20½ in (52 cm) wide. However, there are variations, so work out the surface area of one roll of paper by multiplying the two dimensions together.

Adjust your calculations if entire walls are taken up by picture windows or fitted cabinets. However, doors and other smaller areas that do not need wallpapering should be included, since you will need to make allowances for trimming the paper while fitting around them.

MEASURING TO CUT

Measuring wallpaper to fit is a simple process as long as a few rules are followed. First, measure the height of a required length by measuring the exact distance between the ceiling to the top of the baseboard. Next, the size of the pattern repeat must be added to this measurement and finally an extra 1 in (2.5 cm) must be added at the top and bottom of the length to allow for trimming. With particularly large repeats, this method can produce a lot of wastage. It is often better to hold up a roll of dry paper next to the previously hung length and match it, so that it can be cut precisely and then pasted before it is applied to the wall. For patterns with no repeat, such as stripes, only the allowance for trimming needs to be added to the standard height measurement. This means that with patterns that have little or no repeat, it is easier to cut a number of lengths in readiness for hanging, whereas with larger repeat patterns, it is often easier to cut one length to size at a time.

PASTING PAPER

Wallpapers are divided into two categories: pre-pasted paper with dry paste attached to its backing, which is reactivated by submerging in cold water, and paste-the-back paper, which requires traditional paste to stick it to the wall.

PRE-PASTED PAPER

1 Fill a water trough at the end of the pasting table two-thirds full. Roll up a length of wallpaper, pattern inward, and submerge it for the recommended soaking time.

2 Pull the paper onto the table, folding so that pasted surface meets pasted surface. Repeat this step at the other end of the length. Leave it to soak for the required time.

PASTE-THE-BACK PAPER

1 Roll out the wallpaper along the pasting table. Make sure that the paste is mixed according to the manufacturer's instructions for the type of paper you are using. Apply paste from the center of the paper out toward its edges, ensuring total and even coverage.

2 When the paper is covered with paste, pick up the end of the length and lift and slide it along the pasting table, folding as you progress along the length of it.

3 Continue the folding along the length of pasted paper. Remove the folded length from the table and leave it to soak for the required time before applying to the wall.

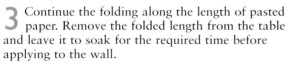

LINING

L ining paper can be applied to walls (especially old, unsound ones) in order to create the best possible surface for the wallpaper. It acts in a similar way to an undercoat before the top coat of paint. Although it is not essential, a lining paper greatly improves a wallpapered finish, and in many cases, manufacturer's guidelines state that lining is vital before applying their wallpaper. Paste is applied to lining paper in the same way as for wallpaper (see page 69).

CEILINGS

Although ceilings are not often wallpapered, they can benefit from being lined. Whether lining a ceiling for wallpapering or painting purposes, make sure that the surface is thoroughly prepared before applying the lining paper and check that the correct sealer or size has been applied.

Using the wall/ceiling junction as the starting point, begin lining. Alternatively, begin in the center of the room in order to bisect a hanging light (see opposite).

Support the paper with one hand while brushing out with the other hand.

Line away from the natural light source in order to make seams less visible.

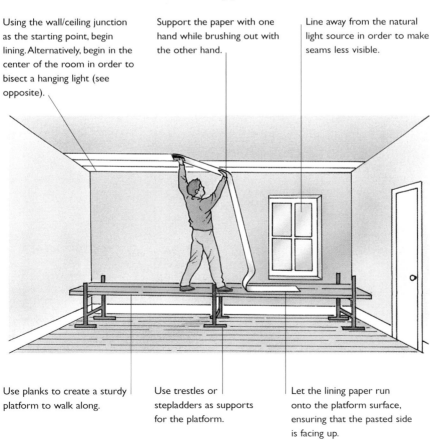

Use planks to create a sturdy platform to walk along.

Use trestles or stepladders as supports for the platform.

Let the lining paper run onto the platform surface, ensuring that the pasted side is facing up.

HANGING GUIDELINES

Ceilings may appear awkward to paper, but they can be easier than walls since they have far fewer obstacles. Beginning each length from a secure starting point is essential for papering ceilings successfully.

1 Brush the start of the length securely into the ceiling/wall junction, allowing a small overlap for trimming. Progress along the length, brushing out air bubbles and joining precisely with the previous length.

3 Brush the trimmed paper back into position, to create a perfect cut edge.

2 At each wall/ceiling junction, pull back the paper and cut along the creased guideline. To make the guideline more visible, you can mark the crease with a pencil before pulling the paper back.

4

DEALING WITH LIGHT FIXTURES

Hanging light fixtures can be dealt with in two different ways, as shown below. Whenever papering around electrical fixtures, ensure that the power is turned off at the electical distribution box before work commences.

Coinciding seams: if the paper will bisect the light, loosen its backing plate and brush the paper behind it.

Threading light: where it meets the light centrally, cut a hole in the paper. Thread the light through; trim.

LINING WALLS

Traditionally, lining paper is applied to walls horizontally, though this is not essential. It is best to apply lining paper so that the fewest possible lengths are used on any particular wall, whether this is vertically or horizontally. This means that large walls are best lined horizontally and small alcoves are best lined vertically. When lining vertically, the one consideration is to make sure that when it comes to wallpapering, the lining paper seams and the wallpaper seams do not coincide. The examples below show how to line walls horizontally; the vertical method can be achieved using the wallpapering guidelines shown later in this chapter.

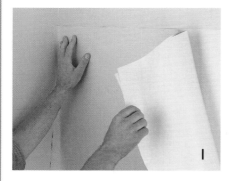

4

1 Join lengths of paper at the corner junction, allowing for a small overlap for trimming purposes. Hold the folded paper in one hand while positioning with the other hand.

2 Using a paperhanging brush, smooth out the length, gradually unrolling the folds and joining the paper with the previous length. Always butt-join the lengths and avoid any overlaps.

3 Trim the paper into the corners, using scissors, or a craft knife as shown here.

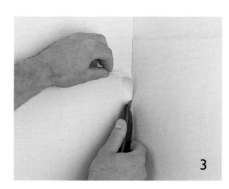

CORNERS

For internal corners, the lining paper should always be trimmed along the corner junction, as shown opposite. External corners require the paper to be molded around the edge of the corner in order to maintain the continuity of a single length. The method demonstrated here will only work if the external corner is square. Where this is not the case, it may be necessary to use the method for dealing with external corners when wallpapering (see page 82).

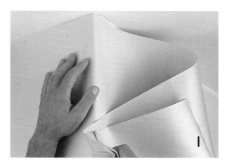

1 Unroll the paper folds, letting the paper bend around the edge of the external corner and onto the adjacent wall.

2 Before brushing the paper out on the adjacent wall, use your fingers to crease along the edge of the corner, smoothing out and removing any air bubbles.

FINISHING OFF

Once the room is lined and the paper has dried, fill any seam gaps with filler to make a perfectly smooth surface for wallpapering. Apply some "size" (diluted wallpaper paste) to the lining paper and leave it to dry—this will make it much easier to hang the wallpaper because it lets the paper slip across the lined surface when you are positioning it.

4

Filling gaps: if there are gaps between seams in the lined surface, apply some fine filler to these areas to make a smooth surface. Sand the area lightly once the filler is dry.

Finishing corners: decorator's caulking around internal corner junctions and joints between lining paper and wood provides an even finish and stops the paper from lifting.

WHERE TO START WALLPAPERING

There are a number of factors to consider when deciding on the best place to begin wallpapering. In order to make sure that the wallpaper will create the best possible effect, you need to take a little time to decide on the most appropriate starting point as well as the best place to finish and join up the pattern as a whole. As room designs and layouts vary dramatically, it is difficult to cover every eventuality here. However, there are a number of points that can be considered as general guidelines when deciding where to begin.

Centralizing: bold patterned papers with large repeats may require the main design in the paper to be centralized on a particular wall in order to create a balanced overall effect. The obvious place would be on a chimney-breast or centrally between two windows on the same wall. With smaller patterns, this process is not as essential as the balance of the design will not be dependent on central positioning.

A complete start: always try to make sure that the first length you hang is a complete uninterrupted drop that requires no intricate trimming. Never trust an internal corner as a vertical starting point—it is best to use a spirit level to ensure that you are starting from a precisely vertical position.

Avoiding finishing with a seam match: where a room does not have a continuous wall surface around the entire circumference of the room, avoid having to join the paper at the end of the job. This avoids the need for what can often be a tricky pattern match in order to finish the room.

4

Marking the position: work out where subsequent lengths of paper will hang by measuring around the circumference of the room with a roll of wallpaper. Mark positions on the wall and adjust accordingly for the most suitable positions for lengths to hang.

THE STARTING POINTS

Centralizing

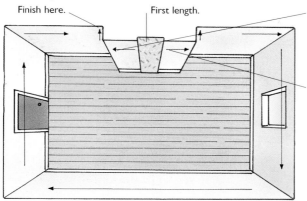

Finish here.   First length.

After the first length, paper around this corner of the chimney-breast.

Continue around the other corner of the chimney-breast and on around the rest of the room.

A complete start

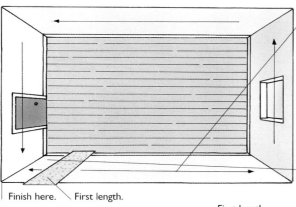

After the first length, continue around the rest of the room.

Final length may need to overlap in the corner to create a joint.

Finish here.   First length.

Avoiding finishing with a seam match

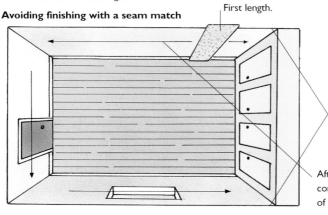

First length.

Finish here.

After the first length, continue around the rest of the room.

4

HANGING THE FIRST LENGTH

H anging the first length correctly is the most important part of creating any wallpaper design, as this initial application forms the base on which the rest of the pattern is built. If the first length is not vertical, this slant will be repeated throughout the entire room, so it is essential to take time to make sure that the first length is straight.

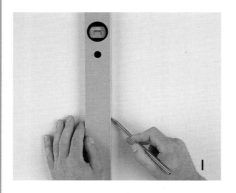

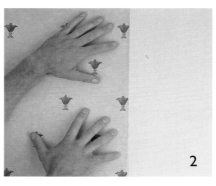

1 At your starting position, draw a pencil line from ceiling to floor, using a level to ensure that it is precisely vertical.

2 Position the first length at the top of the wall, and slide it into place so the edge of the paper runs along the pencil guideline. Allow a small overlap onto the ceiling.

4

3 Crease the top of the paper into the wall/ceiling junction, then brush the paper with a paperhanging brush to remove air bubbles and ensure that the paper is firmly stuck to the wall. Work the bristles of the brush from the center of the length outward and downward.

4 When you reach the bottom of the length, use the paperhanging brush to crease the paper securely into the baseboard junction.

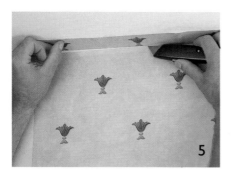

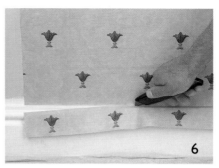

5 Return to the top of the length, then cut along the wall/ceiling junction with a craft knife. Cut slightly above the junction as this tends to give a much neater finish.

6 Brush back down to the bottom of the length and trim the paper with a craft knife, cutting slightly onto the top of the baseboard to produce a clean dividing line.

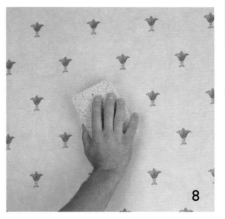

7 Return to the top of the length, then brush all the way down to the bottom again, removing any air bubbles that may have been missed during the initial sweep.

8 Finally, use a sponge rinsed in clean water to wipe over the surface of the entire length of paper to remove any paste residue. Wipe over the adjacent areas of wall and baseboard as well, to ensure that they are paste-free.

JOINING LENGTHS

W hether a wallpaper has a pattern that requires matching or not, adjacent lengths of paper need to be joined very accurately to produce a good finish. The aim should be to butt-join the lengths so that the two pieces form a seam where they meet, without overlapping.

MAKING THE SEAM JOINT

Where the pattern requires precise matching, it is obviously important to make the match between papers as precise as possible. However, some papers are prone to stretching, and some may even have slight variations within a roll, which makes pattern matching difficult. Always try to make the first point of matching at normal eye level in the room; if there are cases where the pattern drops, these inconsistencies will be positioned lower down the wall where they will be far less visible.

4

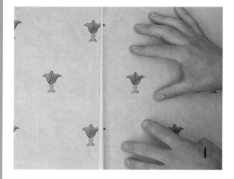

1 Slide the new length up to the previous one, matching the pattern first at eye level and then down the rest of the length. Brush out and trim the length in the usual way.

2 Most papers will join easily, but it may be necessary to run a seam roller lightly down the seams to ensure a good finish.

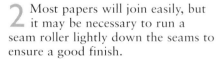

3 Where the edges dry out too quickly, apply some more paste with a fine paintbrush, then stick the paper down again, as required.

TYPES OF MATCH

Wallpaper patterns are matched between lengths using more than one method. It is important to be aware of the subtle differences between the designs as these can affect the way in which pattern matching is achieved. Use the best method for the particular paper you are trying to hang.

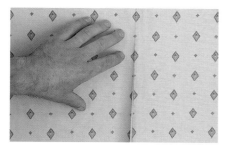

Straight match: the seam for a straight-match pattern is made very simple by having the match bisect a main feature in the design itself— when two pieces of paper are being joined, it is perfectly clear where the second paper should be positioned in order to reunite the pattern.

MISCELLANEOUS MATCHES

Some designers produce papers that have variations on the matches demonstrated here, but in such cases, instructions are usually supplied with the paper. Sometimes, straight-match paper design is slightly "offset" so that joining is not as clear as in most cases. Also, some free-match papers are in fact straight match, which may only become apparent once the paper is hung. Always read the manufacturer's guidelines before hanging a wallpaper, especially when the design is not straightforward.

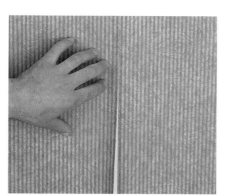

Free match: these are often the easiest papers to join as you don't need to worry about matching the pattern at specific points—it is butt-joined at any point. However, manufacturers often suggest that for papers with a strong overall pattern, every second length should be inverted.

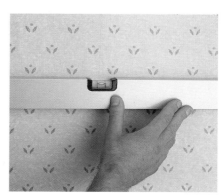

Level match: with some wallpapers the actual match is free, but the paper design of each length needs to be level with the previous one. Once a length has been applied, use a level to check that the whole design remains constant and in the correct position on the wall.

4

INTERNAL CORNERS

A s all rooms have internal corners, learning how to deal with them is an important part of basic papering technique. However square an internal corner is, never try to bend a full length of paper around it because the paper will always wrinkle along the junction, producing an unsightly finish. The best technique is to cut a single length in two and rejoin it precisely along the corner junction.

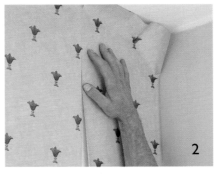

4

1 Measure the exact distance from the last full length to the corner junction. Check this distance along the entire length to make sure there are no slight variations along the junction. Add ½ in (12 mm) to this measurement, and cut the next length of paper into two pieces accordingly.

2 Paste the first length of wallpaper, and pattern match it as usual to the previous length.

3 Brush it into place, allowing for the ½-in (12-mm) overlap to bend around onto the adjacent wall.

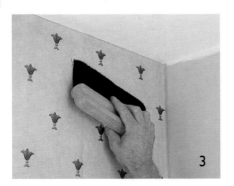

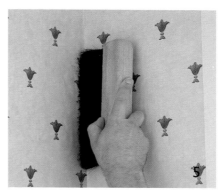

4 Paste the other half of the length of paper and position it on the adjacent wall, matching the pattern as well as possible. Undulations along the corner junction may mean that the match is not exact in some places. However, the length must be hung vertically, so use a spirit level to make sure that it hangs in the correct position on the wall.

5 Make sure that the edge of the second half of the length is firmly stuck down, especially along the corner junction. Trim off any excess paper, as required.

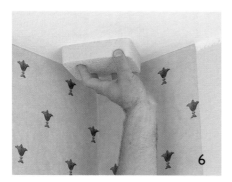

6 Use a clean, dampened sponge to wipe away any excess paste from both the surface of the wallpaper and also from the ceiling and the baseboard, respectively.

7 To ensure that the corner stays stuck down—especially vinyl paper—pull back the edge and apply overlap adhesive along the junction. Push the paper back in position.

4

EXTERNAL CORNERS

The technique for dealing with external corners varies considerably from the one for internal corners. Where these corners are square, it is possible to bend wallpaper around them and continue along the wall as usual. However, in most cases, a length will cease to be level as it rounds the corner, and an alternative technique is required.

1 Bend the wallpaper around the corner and trim to fit as well as possible. Be careful not to let the wallpaper tear at ceiling or baseboard level.

2 Apply a second length of paper, overlapping the first, matching the pattern on the overlap close to the corner. Trim the length to fit.

3 Hold a spirit level vertically in the center of the overlapping lengths, and cut through both pieces of paper using a craft knife. Continue the cut from ceiling to baseboard.

4

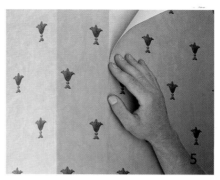

4 Peel back the second length of paper and then remove the two excess strips of wallpaper that have been produced by the cut with the craft knife.

5 Smooth back the second length of paper to produce a perfect butt-joint. It may be necessary to use a seam roller along the joint to produce a perfect flat match.

6 This technique can be very messy and results in a lot of paste getting onto the wallpaper surface. Be sure to remove all of this residue with a clean, damp sponge.

4

EXTERNAL CORNER CONSIDERATIONS

• Cutting: the most important thing to consider is where to create the overlap before cutting through the lengths. This will depend on how far the first length of paper bends around the corner and the most appropriate place to match the pattern. For papers with an open background, it is best to cut through the background rather than the main part of the pattern. For wallpapers with a more complicated or busy design, it is less important where you overlap and cut.

• Keeping level: when matching the second length to the first one, there may need to be some compromise between exact pattern matching and keeping the paper vertical. Ensuring that the paper is precisely vertical is the first priority; after that, join the pattern as accurately as possible, paying particular attention at eye level. Use a level to make sure that the edge of the second length is vertical and can then act as a good starting point for papering the rest of the wall surface.

PROBLEM SOLVING

Most papering problems are due to poor application and general technique, though sometimes a particular paper can be difficult to hang. Whatever the reason, most problems can be overcome or any damage can be repaired—things that require extra work to correct, represent a good lesson for future projects.

4

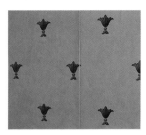

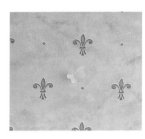

Lifting seams: in any room, it is likely that some seams will dry out and come away from the wall. Simply reapply some paste to the area and stick the paper down again; remove excess paste.

White seams: where dark colors are joined, the lining paper will show through if the seams do not match precisely. Use a fiber-tip pen the same color as the paper to touch-in these areas.

Tearing: wallpaper is vulnerable to tearing just after it has been applied, while it is still wet. Most tears look worse than they are; it is usually possible to tease the paper back in place and stick it down.

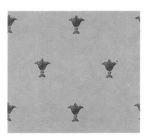

Shiny seams: this is the result of overbrushing the seams during application and/or the presence of paste along the seam. Wash seams with a mild detergent and then rinse with clean water.

Poor pattern match: it may be the case that the paper has stretched so the pattern matches in some areas but not in others. Most small mistakes will not be noticeable, but be more careful in the future.

Bubbles: bubbles occur when wallpaper has not been left for the correct soaking time before applying it to the wall. Small bubbles can be split open and stuck down. Large areas will need to be stripped.

Papering Awkward Areas

5

PAPERING AWKWARD AREAS

Having mastered basic wallpapering techniques, dealing with more complex obstacles on a wall surface becomes progressively easier and less daunting. Most obstacles require trimming around, and this tends to be the difficult part. The secret of wallpapering these areas is precise trimming, which in effect means taking a little extra time when there is a lot of intricate cutting and trimming involved. Creating clear, sharp edges and accurate seams will make the end product far more impressive. For those areas of the home that are an awkward shape, such as stairwells, taking your time is, again, the crucial factor. This way you can keep to the correct work sequence, which, in turn, will produce the best finish.

5

DOORS AND ENTRANCES

A ll rooms have a doorway of some description, so it is essential to know the best way of papering around them. Most doors have a frame or casing, which makes papering much easier; however, some entrances have no doors or frames and these require a different technique altogether.

DOORS

Always ignore the door itself and concentrate on the frame because this has a precise edge to paper up to, which makes papering a straightforward exercise in cutting and trimming.

1 Let the length of paper flop loosely over the corner of the frame, being careful not to tear the paper. Make a diagonal cut back to the corner.

2 Use the paperhanging brush to crease the paper carefully into the frame/wall junction both at the side and above the door.

3 Trim the excess paper with a craft knife, and remove residual paste from the paper and door frame with a damp sponge.

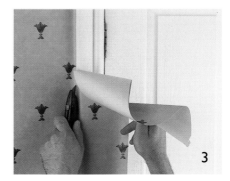

5

ARCHES

An entrance that does not contain a door or frame is more difficult to paper around, especially if it is a curved one, such as an arch. As long as the correct technique is followed, however, it is possible to paper an archway very successfully.

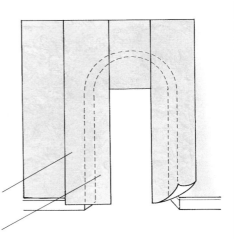

Let lengths of paper on the main wall go over and beyond the edge of the arch.

Trim the paper back to 1 in (2.5 cm) from the edge of the arch.

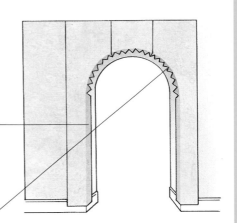

On the straight edges of the arch, bend the paper around the edge, allowing it to stick on the internal wall of the arch.

On the curved edges of the arch, make a number of cuts in the paper at right angles to the edge in order to bend the paper around the edge. The small flaps can then be stuck to the internal edge of the curve.

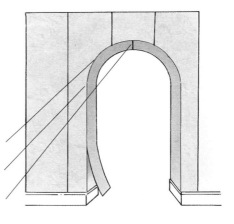

Cut two pieces of paper to run inside the arch.

Ensure a straight edge along the corner junction.

Join the two pieces at the top of the arch.

5

WINDOWS

Windows that are not recessed into the wall, and therefore have no deep sill, can be treated in a similar manner to doors, since the wallpaper is simply trimmed up to the window frame. However, where the window is recessed, the papering technique needs to be adjusted to take into account the edges and corners.

RECESSED WINDOWS

Recessed windows, which are present in many homes, vary in shape and in size, but the technique used to paper around them is the same whatever the shape. Following the correct work sequence and cutting precisely is all that is required to overcome these obstacles.

1 Let the wallpaper go across the recess, making sure that it is also stuck firmly in position on the wall. Use scissors to make a horizontal cut back to the corner of the recess precisely along the top edge of the recess.

2 Make a similar horizontal cut along the bottom edge of the recess, back to the corner of the window sill. It may be necessary to use a craft knife to cut around the corner of the sill to release the required flap of paper above.

3 Bend the flap of paper around the external corner of the recess, creasing it into the frame edge junction. Trim it with a craft knife to fit accurately.

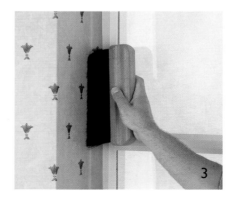

5

4 Apply another length of paper overlapping the previous length. The second length should be just long enough for the bottom edge of it to reach the window frame in the recess when it has been trimmed to fit. Match the pattern very carefully all along the overlap.

5 Use a craft knife and a straightedge (a level is ideal) to cut diagonally through the overlapping lengths of wallpaper, back to the recess corner.

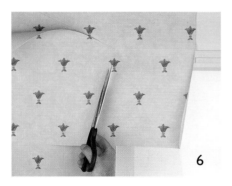

6 Use scissors to trim the bottom section of the second length back to the recess corner and the diagonal cut made in Step 5.

7 Peel back the second length of wallpaper and remove the excess paper below it (the top section of the first length).

8 Smooth the first length back to create a perfect butt-joint and fold the bottom part of the second length under the recess, then trim to the frame, as required. Finally, sponge off excess paste with a damp sponge. Continue along to the other end of the window and repeat the process around the other side of the recess.

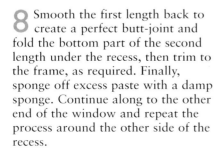

5

WALL SWITCHES AND SOCKETS

E lectrical wall switches and sockets are common obstacles in most rooms so it is important to know the most appropriate technique for wallpapering around them. The technique for wallpapering around switches and power points is the same. As with all electrical fittings, make sure that the power is turned off at the electrical distribution box before you begin to work around them.

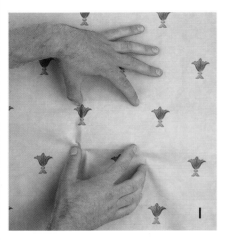

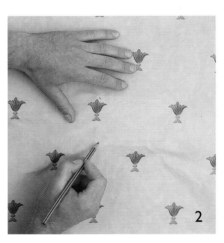

1 Let the paper hang over the front of the switch and carefully mold the paper to its outline, being careful not to make any tears or rips across the paper surface.

2 Make a pencil mark slightly in from each of the four corners.

3 Use scissors to cut four diagonal lines from the center of the switch plate out to the marks. This creates four triangular flaps.

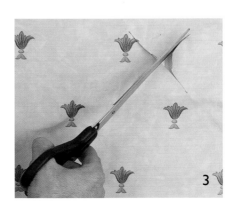

5

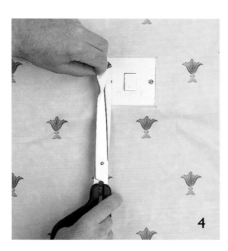

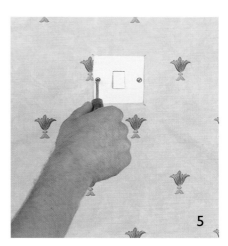

4 Cut away each flap to reveal a square hole in the wallpaper, slightly smaller than the switch plate itself.

5 Loosen the retaining screws on the switch plate until it comes free from the wall surface.

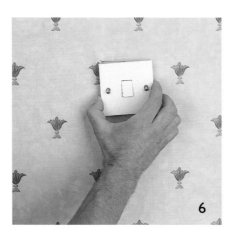

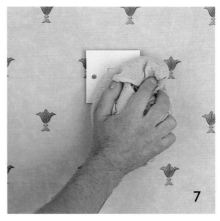

6 By carefully moving the plate into a diagonal position, it is possible to pull it through the square in the wallpaper, allowing the cut edges of the wallpaper to be hidden behind the plate.

7 Tighten up the retaining screws, making sure that the switch plate is level. Use a dry rag to remove any excess paste. Do not turn the electricity back on until the switch is totally dry.

5

WALL OBSTACLES

M ost obstacles encountered along a wall surface can be overcome using the techniques already demonstrated, or by combining techniques. If at all possible, try and remove the obstacle.

DEALING WITH RADIATORS

Radiators are an awkward shape to paper around and they require ingenuity and patience. Remember that the seam behind a radiator will not be seen; the areas to concentrate on are those directly around and just behind the edge.

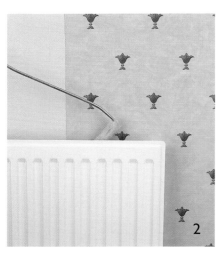

| Let the length of paper hang loosely over the front of the radiator. Cut slits in the paper to correspond with the brackets that support the weight of the radiator.

2 Use a small, long-handled roller to push the paper behind the radiator, positioning it so that the cut in the paper coincides with the position of the supporting bracket.

RADIATOR REMOVAL

Radiators should only be removed if you have some plumbing experience. If a radiator is taken off, remove the brackets but replace screw anchors. Use the paperhanging brush to smooth the paper over the screws, letting them pierce the paper. Unscrew the screws and reattach the bracket; repeat with the next length.

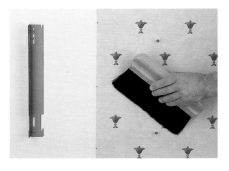

5

MISCELLANEOUS OBSTACLES

For all the other obstacles that may be encountered, common sense and planning are the best tools for successfully wallpapering around them. The guidelines below deal with some of the more common ones.

COMMON OBSTACLES

- Lights: if possible, remove wall lights, paper the area and refit the lights. Remember to turn off the electricity before disconnecting the light.
- Hooks: it is always best to remove hooks before wallpapering, unless you are certain that pictures will be hung back in the same place. A new pattern or design often leads to a different choice of picture, and starting afresh after wallpapering is usually the best policy.
- Phone sockets: these can be treated in the same way as electrical sockets (see page 90). Carefully undo the front plate from a phone socket, then undo the retaining screws that secure it to the wall. Be careful not to dislodge any wires when carrying out this procedure.
- Fireplaces: these are nothing more than intricate moldings, the next stage on from papering around a door frame. Make cuts in the paper at right angles to the fireplace profile then the paper will mold easily around its edge and make it easier to trim with a craft knife.
- Toilets: the tank usually has a curved edge which makes it difficult to trim around accurately. Take the top off the tank, if possible, then apply the paper before replacing the top. This produces a very neat edge at this level. For the sides, trim the paper to slightly less than what appears to be the correct size. The excess paper can then be pushed into the curved junction, creating a neat finish.
- Sinks: these are similar to toilets. However, bear in mind that it is never sensible to wallpaper directly above a sink, since water splashes will soon damage the paper; it is best to tile these areas.
- Wall cabinets: try and remove any wall cabinets before starting to paper, as trimming around them can be a difficult and time-consuming job. Remember to mark fixing holes so the cabinets can be put back once papering is complete.
- Kitchen cabinets: these can be treated in a similar way to wall cabinets since most kitchen wall cabinets can be taken down and repositioned after papering. Floor cabinets are generally permanently fixed. The area directly above countertops is best tiled; if it is wallpapered, the paper will deteriorate rapidly.

5

STAIRWELLS

W orking in stairwells has the problem of access and safety. It is essential to construct a stable, safe platform so that you can reach all those areas that would otherwise be inaccessible. In addition, there are a number of other factors that you need to take into consideration if you are going to achieve the best possible results when wallpapering a stairwell.

STAIRWELL CONSIDERATIONS

- Types of pattern: stairwells are by nature tall and relatively narrow, so consider what effect the wallpaper pattern will have on such an area. Vertical stripes, for example, will make the stairwell appear even taller.

- Two people: the ideal setup for papering a stairwell is to have one person positioning the paper at the top while a second person holds the paper away from the wall at the bottom. You can do it on your own but having two people makes the job a lot easier.

- Using a level: when applying the first length in a stairwell, use a spirit level to check that the paper is vertical up and down the entire length. Long lengths have a tendency to swerve at the bottom even if they are totally vertical at the top.

- Wall bannister: try and remove any bannister or rails from walls that are to be papered, otherwise they

will make the task much more difficult. Reattach them once the papering is complete.

- Adjust the platform: not all stairwell designs are like the one shown opposite. Where necessary, adjust platforms with extra ladders and planks to account for turns in the staircase, or more complicated designs than a simple straight run of stairs.

- Soaking times: be accurate and consistent with the time you leave the wallpaper to soak after it has been pasted and before it goes on the wall. Fluctuating these times from length to length can cause pattern matching problems, which will be accentuated over the long seams in a stairwell.

THE STAIRWELL SETUP

Designs vary, but safety should always be the primary concern when building a platform in a stairwell. Make sure that all the equipment you are using is in good condition and able to withstand the stresses that will be put on it.

Position of first drop—work away from this length both at the top and lower level of the stairs.

Use rope to bind the plank to the ladder and stepladder.

Paper once side walls are finished.

Use padding on top of the ladder to protect the wall surface.

Depending on the length requirement and thickness of the plank, more support may be needed here.

5

BORDERS

B orders add a decorative edge to a wall finish. They can either be an addition to the wallpaper design itself or they can be applied on a plain painted wall to add a patterned frame to the overall finish. Application methods vary according to where the border is being used.

CEILING LEVEL

Ceiling level is the easiest place to hang a border because the ceiling junction can be used as a guideline when positioning the border itself. All borders should be pasted using proprietary border adhesive, which is stronger than standard paste and adheres much better to the wall surface.

1 Continue the ceiling color slightly onto the wall surface so that if there are any undulations in the ceiling junction it will not be possible to see any wall color above the border when it is applied—this gives the appearance of a precisely level ceiling edge.

2 Fold up the border in a similar way as to when hanging wallpaper. Apply the border using the ceiling junction as a guide to positioning the top edge of the border. Use a paperhanging brush to smooth the border and remove any air bubbles from under its surface.

Applying on wallpaper: the advantage of applying a border on wallpaper is that it is usually easy to keep the border level by following a line in the actual pattern of the wallpaper. Where there is no ordered pattern to follow, draw a pencil guideline, as shown opposite.

5

PICTURE AND DADO BORDERS

Applying a border in one of the central areas of a wall is a simple process as long as the border is kept precisely level. When dealing with internal corners, never try to bend a single length around the corner as it will invariably shrink slightly as it dries and pull away from the corner junction. Use a single length of border per wall; join each length, matching the pattern along the junction.

1 Make a pencil mark on the wall at the required level and use a spirit level to draw a line around the entire perimeter of the room.

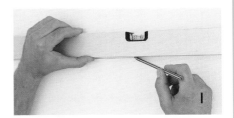

2 Use the pencil line as a guide for hanging the border. Crease the border firmly into the corner and trim it so that it overlaps slightly onto the adjacent wall.

3 Apply a second length of border so that it overlaps onto the first, being careful to match the pattern precisely. Draw a pencil guideline along the junction, peel the border back and trim with scissors.

4 Smooth the border back in place and remove the excess paste with a clean, damp sponge.

TRIMMING CORNERS

Use scissors to trim the border at the corner instead of a craft knife. A craft knife blade might cut through both strips of border, which would mean that once the borders were brushed back in place, the ends would not meet at the corner.

5

COMBINING PAPERS

R ather than using just one wallpaper to decorate a room, it is possible to combine different papers to create an interesting and varied effect. Many manufacturers produce papers with this idea in mind and coordinate borders to be used with specific papers. You can either follow their guidelines or you can create your own individual schemes.

Using a border divide: using two different papers on the same wall surface requires some sort of border to divide the two patterns. A paper border acts as an ideal dado divide, separating the designs while adding a decorative feature.

Solid borders: a solid wooden dado trim can be used to divide different papers. This provides a pronounced finish and a clear-cut edge to both the wallpapers.

Framing: borders and wallpaper can be combined to create framed areas along a wall surface. The technique for creating mitered corner seams in borders is explained on page 111.

5

Combining Paper and Paint

6

COMBINING PAPER AND PAINT

A successful decorative finish depends on a good combination of color and design. By blending paper and paint together you can produce a very attractive and balanced decorative scheme. Texture and color can each create stunning results, and by combining the media of paint and paper, the options for experimentation are increased. There are many ways in which they can be combined and this chapter illustrates just a few of them, so you can go on to develop your own original ideas for all kinds of interesting and unique finishes.

WHAT TO USE WHERE

Different paint and paper combinations can be used in particular areas of the home to create highly decorative effects. However, it is worthwhile bearing in mind that some combinations and effects are better suited to certain areas than others.

SUITING DIFFERENT AREAS

- Stairwells: these tend to receive a lot of wear and tear at the lower levels but not at the top. This makes them an ideal area to have a wooden dado trim dividing two papers, or to have paper above the trim and paint below. Then, when the bottom level becomes worn, it can be redecorated while the top level is left as it is.

- Child's bedroom: in a similar manner to stairwells, the bottom level of the wall surface tends to get damaged more quickly. Having a wooden dado trim divide or a paper border means that the bottom level can be redecorated while the top level is left untouched. A paint effect below the dado trim can also help to disguise blemishes and make the finish last as long as possible.

- Alcoves: these offer the opportunity to create a feature within a room, and can be treated differently to the rest of the decoration in the room. If the main walls are wallpapered, the back of the alcoves can be painted a light color. This gives the effect of greater depth and provides an ideal background for displaying ornaments.

- Paper panels: paper panels can be very effective on

walls, but they are less common on wooden surfaces. However, panel doors offer an ideal opportunity for using wallpaper in a different way since the central area of each panel can be wallpapered to match the walls while the rest of the door is painted to match the other woodwork in the room.

- Decoupage: this technique involves cutting out attractive designs or shapes from wallpaper, or other sources, and sticking them to the wall to create a collage effect. It is a good way of faking images, which is usually the domain of faux or trompe l'oeil artists.

- Painted borders: using paint as a border is another alternative to wooden dado trim or paper borders. Painted borders can be applied at any level to produce a frame for a particular feature.

PAINTABLE PAPERS

Textured and paintable papers are the crossover between the wallpapering and painting worlds. These types of paper usually have an embossed surface, which adds depth to the finish once the paper is applied to the wall. The textured pattern is excellent for covering up rough wall surfaces since the undulations are obscured by the thick embossed nature of the paper. Some textured papers can be left unpainted, although most will benefit from being painted in either light or dark colors.

Keeping it simple: a textured patterned paper can be painted a light color while still showing off the depth in design. Using the paper up to the dado level also breaks up the wall surface, providing greater character and impact.

Adding color: textured papers can be painted bold colors to enhance their features while at the same time creating a very solid look. Painted with vinyl latex, this effect is very hardwearing and easy to clean.

Basic texture: woodchip paper is one of the most common of all the textured papers and is extremely good for covering old, uneven walls. On its own, the effect can be very ordinary, but with the right accessories, woodchip paper can become an attractive integral part of a decorative scheme.

6

HANGING TEXTURED PAPERS

Textured papers are hung in a similar way to standard wallpaper, but with one or two subtle differences in technique. Because they are generally heavier, the soaking time for textured paper tends to be slightly longer, and the paste is usually mixed to a stronger, thicker consistency.

EMBOSSED PAPERS

Embossed papers have a relief pattern that raises the design, giving a much greater feeling of depth to the paper finish. When applying these types of wallpaper, care must be taken not to flatten the relief pattern and damage the textured effect.

1 Check the ends of each roll of wallpaper to make sure that the edges are not damaged.

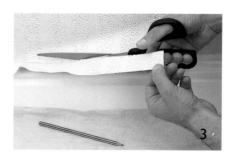

2 Once the paper has been pasted and left to soak for the manufacturer's recommended time, apply it to the wall using a paperhanging brush. Be careful not to brush the paper too much, especially along the seams.

3 Trim the lengths with scissors— the coarse texture of the paper tends to blunt craft knife blades very quickly, and a blunt blade can lead to the paper being torn.

6

WOODCHIP REPAIRS

Textured woodchip paper is ideal for old, uneven walls because it covers and disguises imperfections in the surface. As with embossed papers, use scissors for trimming—the small pieces of wood fiber in the paper are difficult to cut through with a craft knife. The most versatile property of woodchip paper is that it is very easy to repair damaged areas simply by patching and repainting.

1 Use a scraper to remove the loosely stuck down edges of the damaged area of woodchip paper.

2 Cut a piece of woodchip paper slightly larger than the hole. Hold it against the damaged area, tearing around the circumference of the hole as accurately as possible.

3 Apply paste to the new patch of woodchip paper and stick it in place over the hole.

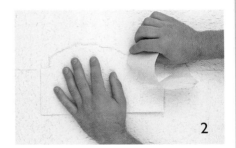

4 Once the patch has dried, paint over the whole area to complete the repair job.

6

PAINT EFFECTS ON TEXTURED PAPER

Textured papers offer the opportunity to create excellent paint effects since the raised surface adds an extra dimension to the finished product. Applying the effect to the high points will give an entirely different finish from applying it to the low points of the paper.

COLOR WIPING

Color wiping is a method of coloring the low points of a textured paper. It gives the appearance of the base color being ingrained with the glaze color that is applied to create the effect. Use a vinyl latex paint as the base coat for this paint effect.

1 Apply the glaze generously in all directions across the surface of the textured paper.

2 Use a clean, damp sponge to wipe down the paper in long vertical sweeps. This technique is best used on papers with a dominant vertical pattern, as shown here; however, for an all-over design, the sponge can be wiped across the surface of the paper in any direction.

LEAVING THE PEAKS
The finished effect leaves the peaks on the textured wallpaper surface clear of glaze so that the base coat color shows clearly on these raised areas.

COLOR HIGHLIGHTING

The aim of highlighting is to accentuate the peaks in the paper with the glaze color, rather than the troughs. The glaze is applied to the peaks and left in place, rather than being wiped away as with the color wiping technique. A base coat of vinyl latex paint should be used for this effect as well.

1 Once the brush has been dipped in glaze, dry off the excess from the bristles with a clean rag.

2 Use light sweeping horizontal strokes across the surface of the paper, letting the bristles touch just the top of the relief pattern.

3 Build up the depth of color to the level you require before moving on to the next area on the paper surface.

TEXTURE WITH HEIGHT AND DEPTH
The result looks as if the paper texture has both height and depth—very different from the effect of color wiping, even though the same glaze, paper, and base coat have been used to achieve this highlighting.

6

HANGING WALL PANELS

Wall panels are thicker than wallpaper and require a heavy-duty paste in order to stick them to the wall. To produce the best possible finish, walls should also be lined before applying the panels. Most panels are designed to be applied at dado level around a room. It is usually possible to apply whole panels and reduce the need for cutting and trimming.

1 Soak the back of the wall panel with warm water, and leave for 20 minutes before applying paste. This lets the panel expand, and will prevent any bubbles from appearing in its surface later.

2 Apply paste generously to the panel, ensuring that it covers all areas including the edges.

3 Apply the panel to the wall, ideally starting in an internal corner. Use a spirit level to ensure that the panel is vertical.

4 Brush out any air bubbles in the paper using a paperhanging brush. Be careful not to damage the panel surface during this process.

6

5 Once one wall is complete, begin the adjacent wall. Start, and therefore join, the design at the internal corner.

6 Run a bead of decorator's caulking along internal corners to produce a perfect neat finish.

CUTTING REQUIREMENTS

When smaller panels are required, use a straightedge and craft knife to cut the panel to the correct size before pasting.

WALL PANEL BORDERS

You can enhance the wall panel effect by adding a border or dado rail above it. Paper borders are not ideal for this purpose as they tend to be overshadowed by the depth of the wall panels themselves. The solution is to use a border made from the same heavy-duty material as the panels. This should be applied using the same adhesive as that used for the wall panels. The alternative option is to apply a wooden dado rail around the top of the wall panels. This provides a very solid and substantial edge to the complete panel effect. A wooden dado rail can either be painted or stained, according to personal taste.

6

PAINT EFFECTS ON WALL PANELS

W all panels can be painted in a single color or they can be used for various paint effects. In the example below, an impressive verdigris effect has been created by color wiping and highlighting.

1 The texture of wall panels means that both color-wiping and highlighting techniques are ideal to use on them. Clean all the panels with mineral spirits, then let them dry before applying any paint. With ornate panel textures, such as the one shown here, pay particular attention to all the details in the pattern, so that all impurities are removed from the surface. Wear protective gloves to protect your hands.

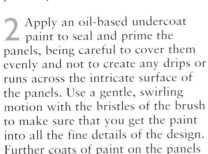

2 Apply an oil-based undercoat paint to seal and prime the panels, being careful to cover them evenly and not to create any drips or runs across the intricate surface of the panels. Use a gentle, swirling motion with the bristles of the brush to make sure that you get the paint into all the fine details of the design. Further coats of paint on the panels can be water-based.

3 A pale green base coat is the ideal color to begin a verdigris effect. As with the undercoat paint, it should be applied all over the wall panel surface. Water-based latex paint is the the best choice. It means that two coats can be applied in one day. Once the second coat is dry, you can begin applying the verdigris effect.

6

4 Load a mini roller with dark green paint, then remove the excess on a piece of scrap paper. Run the roller very gently across the panel surface, just touching the high points and peaks of the pattern. Do not apply too much pressure, otherwise the paint will be forced into the deeper troughs that make up the texture of the panel.

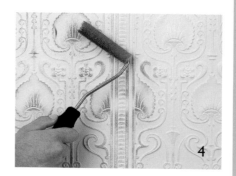

5 Using the same technique as in Step 4, add another coat of paint—with a rusty red being the ideal choice of color. Again, be careful not to apply too much pressure. Try to vary the intensity of the color by applying slightly more paint in some places than in others.

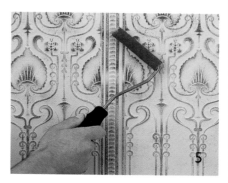

6 Mix a dark green glaze and brush it over the entire panel surface, giving a translucent top coat to the finished effect. Make sure that the entire surface is evenly coated.

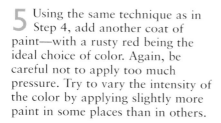

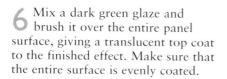

THE VERDIGRIS EFFECT
The finished panel effect can be stunning, providing the perfect background for furniture and ornaments alike. Extra coats of glaze can be applied to create greater depth and texture.

6

FRAMING WITH BORDERS

A s well as creating a decorative edge, borders can be used to very good effect as frames. You can use paint or paper borders to highlight the overall decoration in a room, or they can be used on a smaller scale to accentuate particular features.

PAINTED BORDERS

Using paint to act as a frame is a common concept—in effect, painted door and window frames and baseboards act as the border around walls in most rooms in the house. However, the framed effect can be made more striking by using stencils specifically designed and made for use as a continuous painted border. Using borders in a less obvious position, such as around the baseboard, can create an excellent effect, especially if continued along corner junctions and next to the ceiling so that the entire wall is framed.

1 Use masking tape to stick the stencil to the wall above the baseboard. Make sure that it is level before applying any paint with a stencil brush.

2 Use a second color to add texture to the stenciled border.

3 Move the stencil along and use the last section in the design as a guide for positioning the first section of the stencil on the wall, ready for the next length of border to be stenciled in.

6

PAPER BORDERS

Paper borders can be just as effective as paint in framing walls or areas such as the door frame, as shown below. In addition to the standard technique for applying a border, it is necessary to make mitered seams in the border so that the direction can be changed to produce square 90 degree corners. Choose the borders carefully when planning to make mitered seams, since some border patterns are not suitable for doing this.

1 Apply two lengths of border so that they overlap at the corner of the door frame. When cutting the lengths, allow a generous amount for the overlap. This allows you enough room to maneuver the two strips into the best possible position for matching the pattern and mitering the corner.

2 Use a craft knife to cut through the overlap at a diagonal angle, beginning at the corner of the door frame and finishing at the corner cross section of the two lengths of border. Be careful to avoid cutting the painted wall with the craft knife.

3 Peel back both strips of border and remove the excess pieces of paper created by the diagonal cut. These two pieces are now excess to requirements and can be discarded.

4 Smooth the two strips back into position to produce a neat mitered seam. Remove excess paste with a clean, damp sponge. Use the same technique to deal with the opposite corner of the door frame.

6

INDEX

All illustrations by Chris Forsey. All photographs by Tim Ridley except for the following pages:

l = left, r = right, c = centre, t = top, b = bottom

Page 5 Elizabeth Whiting & Associates; 6t Elizabeth Whiting & Associates; 7t Elizabeth Whiting & Associates; 8t Elizabeth Whiting & Associates; 8c Elizabeth Whiting & Associates; 13t Elizabeth Whiting & Associates, 13c Elizabeth Whiting & Associates; 66t Nick Huggins/Houses & Interiors; 66c Elizabeth Whiting & Associates, 66b Elizabeth Whiting & Associates; 98t Elizabeth Whiting & Associates, 98c Elizabeth Whiting & Associates; 101t Elizabeth Whiting & Associates, 101c Elizabeth Whiting & Associates, 101b Elizabeth Whiting & Associates.